modern
fighter aircraft

modern fighter aircraft

an illustrated history of
war planes from 1945
to the present day

featuring photographs
from the imperial
war museum

francis crosby
of the imperial war museum duxford

southwater

This book is dedicated to my wife Vanessa and daughter Gemma,
for their help and understanding while I was engrossed in writing this,
and to my parents who always encouraged me to learn.

This edition is published by Southwater

Southwater is an imprint of Anness Publishing Ltd
Hermes House, 88–89 Blackfriars Road, London SE1 8HA
tel. 020 7401 2077; fax 020 7633 9499
www.southwaterbooks.com; info@anness.com

© Anness Publishing Ltd 2004

UK agent: The Manning Partnership Ltd,
6 The Old Dairy, Melcombe Road, Bath BA2 3LR;
tel. 01225 478444; fax 01225 478440;
sales@manning-partnership.co.uk

UK distributor: Grantham Book Services Ltd,
Isaac Newton Way,
Alma Park Industrial Estate,
Grantham, Lincs NG31 9SD;
tel. 01476 541080; fax 01476 541061;
orders@gbs.tbs-ltd.co.uk

North American agent/distributor: National Book Network,
4501 Forbes Boulevard, Suite 200, Lanham, MD 20706;
tel. 301 459 3366; fax 301 429 5746; www.nbnbooks.com

Australian agent/distributor: Pan Macmillan Australia, Level 18,
St Martins Tower, 31 Market St, Sydney, NSW 2000; tel. 1300 135
113; fax 1300 135 103; customer.service@macmillan.com.au

New Zealand agent/distributor: David Bateman Ltd,
30 Tarndale Grove, Off Bush Road, Albany, Auckland;
tel. (09) 415 7664; fax (09) 415 8892

Publisher: Joanna Lorenz
Editorial Director: Judith Simons
Project Editor: Felicity Forster
Designer: Steve West

Jacket Design: Balley Design Associates
Copy Editors: Peter Moloney and
Alan Thatcher
Production Controller: Darren Price

Previously published as part of a larger volume, *Fighter Aircraft*

1 3 5 7 9 10 8 6 4 2

PAGE 1: **Saab Gripen.** PAGES 2–3: **Eurofighter Typhoon.** BELOW: **BAE Systems Harriers.**

Contents

Introduction

"It is not to be expected that aircraft will be able to carry out their duties undisturbed. In war, advantages must be fought for and the importance of aerial reconnaissance is so great that each side will strive to prevent the other side making use of it." Royal Flying Corps manual, 1914.

This observation predates the first true fighter aircraft but neatly sums up how fighter aircraft came to be. From simple beginnings over the bloody trenches of World War I, fighter aircraft have developed into the extraordinarily complex machines in service today. Fighters were once biplanes with speeds of 150kph/93mph and a service ceiling of 4265m/ 14,000ft which could be achieved after perhaps 25 minutes of steady climbing. Today's F-15 can climb to 15,250m/50,000ft in a minute and traverse the sky at 2655kph/1650mph.

Although air fighting is only a phenomenon of the last century, it is now central to securing military victory on the ground. Lessons learned in World War II shaped tactics still in place with military strategists today. Bombing raids against enemy positions as a prelude to fighting for air supremacy typify the approach to most modern conflicts. The bomber aircraft would be protected by fighters, and it is the fighters of opposing forces that do battle to gain control of the air over a war zone.

ABOVE: **The F/A-18 Hornet, one of the most capable combat aircraft, can shift from fighter to strike mode on the same mission at the flick of a switch.**
BELOW: **The Soviet MiG-15 was designed with the benefit of swept-wing research captured from the Germans at the end of World War II and was powered by an illegally copied Rolls-Royce Nene turbojet.**

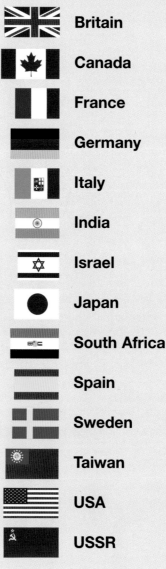

Key to flags

For the specification boxes, the national flag that was current at the time of the aircraft's use is shown.

- Britain
- Canada
- France
- Germany
- Italy
- India
- Israel
- Japan
- South Africa
- Spain
- Sweden
- Taiwan
- USA
- USSR

In the years immediately following the end of World War II, the piston-engined fighter was largely replaced by jet-powered aircraft, although early straight-wing jet fighters were essentially aircraft designed with piston engines in mind. As fighter speeds increased, designers considered aerodynamic refinements such as swept wings. As a consequence of the high speeds, greater stresses were placed on the airframe, so new materials and construction techniques had to be developed.

Guns came to be largely replaced by missiles, initially unguided but today very sophisticated weapons that can seek out and destroy an enemy aircraft from many miles away in most weathers. The other significant development is that of on-board radar equipment, which enables fighter crews to look for hostile aircraft or anti-aircraft installations and then avoid or engage them as appropriate. Although fighter speeds continued to increase throughout the 1950s and 60s, today agility and survivability are considered to be just as important.

This book attempts to tell the story of fighter aircraft and how they evolved, and highlights particular episodes of history in which fighters have played a key role, such as the Korean War and the Gulf War. The A–Z listing of fighters was difficult to compile and does not claim to include every modern fighter built. Instead it presents the individual stories of what the author believes to be the most significant fighters. Specification tables are presented in a consistent manner to enable the reader to readily compare the size, weights and

TOP: **The McDonnell Douglas F-4 Phantom typified the 1950s trend for higher and faster flying fighters.** ABOVE: **The unique V/STOL Harrier gave military leaders the capability to operate fighters from virtually anywhere.** LEFT: **Bristling with air-to-air missiles, the Saab Gripen is one of the world's most modern fighters.**

capability of aircraft as diverse as the Sea Fury, the Shooting Star and the Eurofighter Typhoon.

The performance figures quoted in the table for each type should be seen as a broad indicator of an aircraft's capabilities. Aircraft performance and capability can vary considerably even within the same marks of an aircraft type. If drop tanks are fitted, for example, maximum speed can be reduced – even radio aerials can affect performance. Also, the maximum speeds quoted are top speeds achieved at the optimum altitude for that particular aircraft type and should not be seen as the definitive top speed for an aircraft at all altitudes.

The History of Modern Fighters

The fighter aircraft, born in World War I, has played a crucial role in modern history and continues to make history today. Fighter aircraft have won wars, possibly prevented wars and defended nations from aggressors. Multi-role fighters of today can range over vast areas and unleash a range of "smart" weaponry against the enemy. This is a far cry from the first pistol shots exchanged between "scout" aircraft over the trenches of World War I.

This book tells the story of modern fighter aircraft, how they evolved from the first machines venturing into high-speed flight to the aircraft today that can routinely fly at twice the speed of sound. Particular episodes of history in which fighters have played a key role will be highlighted, such as the Korean War and the Gulf War.

Control of the air alone cannot win wars, as was shown in Vietnam, but without it a war almost certainly cannot be won. Fighter aircraft today can be used to protect national airspace, escort bomber aircraft on hazardous missions and, with the dawn of true multi-role aircraft, carry out reconnaissance or ground-attack missions themselves. As long as air superiority is a military necessity, there will be fighters.

LEFT: **The Panavia Tornado has been the backbone of the Royal Air Force's air defence capability since the late 1980s.**

Higher and faster

By the end of World War II, the piston-engined fighter had effectively been developed to the limits of its possibilities. The future lay with a greater knowledge of aerodynamics and fighters with jet power. Less than a decade after the end of the war, there were fighter aircraft on the drawing board that were planned to travel at up to three times the speed of sound. But jet propulsion also opened up new horizons for bomber aircraft design. While bombers were designed to go higher and faster, fighters were also developed to go higher and faster to intercept and destroy them. Speeds that man had only dreamed of were now within reach.

Whereas propellers would not have looked out of place on some early straight-wing jet fighters, aerodynamicists began to understand more about the special design requirements of high-speed jet aircraft. Wartime German research had found that by sweeping back the wings and tailplanes, the buffeting, vibration and drag experienced by early jets near the speed of sound could be reduced. Designers hoped that this feature could help the aircraft ease through the Mach 1 sound barrier.

TOP: **The Panavia Air Defence Tornado is capable of patrolling and defending huge expanses of airspace.** ABOVE: **The BAC Lightning reached RAF units in 1960. It was the fastest British fighter ever.**

At the same time the experts were trying to get their aircraft higher and higher. The fast climb was essential because it gave defending fighters the chance to reach the "high ground" from which to mount the most effective attack on enemy fighters and bombers – the aim of fighter pilots since World War I.

During the Korean War of 1950–3, the North American F-86 Sabre and the MiG-15 represented the state of the art and both had been designed with the benefit of wartime German research data. Both of these highly successful fighters tried to use their performance to achieve a height advantage

LEFT: **The F-16 has a maximum speed of 2125kph/1320mph and a ceiling in excess of 15,250m/50,000ft which it can reach in one minute.**
BELOW: **The ubiquitous MiG-21, still widely deployed today, was one of the first high-performance all-weather fighters.**

ABOVE: **Much of the performance data of the Saab Gripen remains secret.**

over the enemy, with the result that most fighter actions were fought 8–13km/5–8 miles above the ground. The Korean War had shown that the straight-wing jets had had their day and that high-performance and therefore the most effective fighters would have swept wings and other aerodynamic innovations.

Third-generation jet fighters such as the F-100 Super Sabre and MiG-19 were the first production jet fighters capable of supersonic speeds in level flight but were still essentially fair-weather fighters. It was not until the next wave of jet fighters that the interceptor was born. High-performance fast-climbing aircraft such as the MiG-21 and F-104 could reach speeds of Mach 2 and operate in all weathers.

The 1950s was the golden age of the strategic bomber – the USA, USSR and Britain all had fleets of long-range strategic bombers. High-performance, fast-climbing radar-equipped interceptors such as the English Electric Lightning and Convair F-102 appeared, and in the case of the Lightning could climb at 15,240m/50,000ft per minute.

In 1957 Britain's Defence Minister, Duncan Sandys, said the manned fighter would soon be a thing of the past, replaced by missiles. While this debate raged in the UK, elsewhere larger, often two-seat, fighters armed with missiles were in favour.

While Mach 2 performance and rapid climb are taken for granted in modern fighters, manoeuvrability is just as important. Modern interceptors like the Tornado ADV, F-16 and Gripen have an advantage over even slightly older fighters in that although they have to be able to climb quickly to high altitudes, the pilots don't actually have to see the enemy target aircraft. The powerful radars carried by today's fighters can pick up "bogies" over great distances and air-to-air missiles can be launched at targets beyond visual range.

11

Korea: the first jet v. jet war

Although jet fighter aircraft did enter service with Germany, Britain and the United States towards the end of World War II, it was not until the Korean War of 1950–3 that jet fought jet in the first major air war since World War II. When the war broke out following the North Korean invasion of South Korea on June 25, 1950, both sides were equipped with piston-powered aircraft, the North Korean Air Force having among other combat aircraft a total of 70 aged Soviet Yakovlev Yak-9 fighters. The Communist aggression against South Korea, whose air arm consisted of 16 unarmed trainers, drew the United States and the United Nations to the aid of the South.

The early days of the air war saw World War II types like F- (formerly P-) 51 Mustangs taking on Lavochkin La-7s although the USAF quickly deployed the F-80, the USAF's main fighter in the theatre. This straight-winged jet arrived just too late to see action in World War II but by 1950 was virtually obsolete. Nevertheless it began to rack up significant numbers of kills against the older North Korean types.

On July 3, US Navy jets flew in anger for the first time ever as F9F-3 Panthers escorted a bombing mission. Although the Panther too was a straight-wing jet, it remained the standard US Navy fighter throughout the conflict.

And so for the first six months of the war, the UN were to retain the upper hand in the air and on the ground. But then on November 1, 1950 some USAF Mustang pilots reported coming under fire by six swept-wing jet fighters that had flown across the Yalu river from Manchuria – the Russian-built Mikoyan-Gurevich MiG-15 was in the Korean War. The first jet against jet air combat soon followed on November 8, when four MiGs were seen to fly into Korean air space and were challenged by F-80Cs of the 51 Fighter-Interceptor Wing. Lt Russell J. Brown attacked and destroyed one of the MiGs in mid-air. This historic combat was followed next day by the first jet kill by a US Navy jet when a Panther flown by Lt Commander W.T. Amen shot down another MiG-15. The Russian jets were starting to enjoy victories of their own against USAF B-29 bombers which had previously operated in relative safety. Flying from Chinese bases immune from UN attack, the MiGs were used to defend North Korean installations and represented a major threat to UN air superiority in the north where they created the very dangerous "MiG Alley". UN aircraft could range across the battlefields but faced deadly opposition when they neared areas in range of the MiG bases.

The USAF were quick to respond to the MiG threat and on November 8 ordered the F-86 Sabre-equipped 4th Fighter Group from the USA to Korea. The 27th Fighter-Escort Wing and their F-84 Thunderjets followed soon after. The F-86A was the most modern USAF fighter available but was later shown

TOP: **Two classic jet fighters – the F-86 Sabre (left) and MiG-15.** ABOVE: **Royal Navy Lt Peter Carmichael on the day he downed a MiG jet with his piston-powered Sea Fury.**

TOP: **The F-51 Mustang was widely deployed by the USAF in the early days of the air war.** ABOVE: **A Sea Fury FB Mk II of No.804 Sqdn. Royal Navy leaves the deck of HMS *Glory*.** LEFT: **The remarkable F-82 Twin Mustang was among the first USAF aircraft to operate over Korea.**

to have a slightly inferior performance to that of the MiG. The Sabre's armament of six 12.7mm/0.5in machine-guns was no match for the two 23mm/0.9in and one 37mm/1.46in cannon of the MiG although the Sabre was a steadier gun platform. Tactically, the Communist pilots did themselves no favours, preferring to fly in gaggles of 20 or more aircraft compared to the section of four favoured by Western tacticians.

The first Sabre versus MiG air battle occurred on December 17, 1950 when four F-86s came upon four MiGs at an altitude of 7620m/25,000ft. Lt Colonel Bruce H. Hinton, leader of the F-86 section, fired 1500 rounds of ammunition and sent one MiG down to its destruction. On December 22, eight Sabres took on 15 MiGs and in the dogfights that followed from 9145m/30,000ft down to 305m/1000ft, the USAF pilots destroyed no fewer than six of the MiGs.

The Royal Australian Air Force, initially equipped with F-51 Mustangs, converted to Gloster Meteor F.8s but they were no match for the fast and manoeuvrable MiGs, which inflicted unacceptable losses on the F.8s.

The Republic F-84 Thunderjet was widely used in the war as a fighter-bomber and is credited with a number of air-kills, the first of which came on January 21, 1951. During a dive-bombing attack, F-84s were bounced by MiGs and in the dogfights that followed, Lt Colonel William E. Bertram scored the F-84's first MiG kill.

The MiGs did well to avoid all UN aircraft, not just the jets. The Hawker Sea Fury, operated by the Royal Navy, is known to have destroyed more Communist aircraft than any other non-US type and even shot down a number of North Korean MiGs. During August 1952, while flying the piston-engined Sea Fury off HMS *Ocean*, Royal Navy Lt Peter Carmichael destroyed a MiG-15 jet and earned himself a place in history.

By the end of the Korean War, USAF Sabres had achieved 757 victories for 103 losses. The first jet versus jet war was over and had demonstrated that tactics were as vital as effective weaponry. Straight-winged jets such as the F-80, F-84 and Meteor were shown to have had their day and the swept-winged fighters were on the ascendancy.

Fighter aircraft technology: 1945 to the present day

For most of the latter half of the 20th century, the designers of fighter aircraft continued to do what their predecessors had done – improve performance through more powerful engines and a better understanding of aerodynamics. Piston-engined fighters had virtually reached the end of their evolutionary line by 1945 although many remained in service for some years after the end of World War II. Jet powered fighters began to make their mark toward the end of the war, and within a decade supersonic speeds were regularly achieved, albeit in dives.

A greater understanding of "area rule" – the design technique that produces a fuselage contour with the lowest possible transonic wave drag – came in the 1950s and helped aircraft designers break through the "sound barrier" and produce aircraft capable of supersonic speeds in level flight. The quest for performance as opposed to manoeuvrability was typified by the Lockheed F-104 Starfighter that first flew in 1954.

Jet engine technology progressed rapidly in the 1950s resulting in engines like the F-104's General Electric 7076kg/15,600lb afterburning thrust J79 turbojet. This engine generated more than twice the output of the F-86 Sabre's 3402kg/7500lb thrust J47 turbojet. Compare them both to the 11,340kg/25,000lb thrust engines that power the F-15s in service today. Afterburner or reheat capability was developed in the late 1940s to give fighters an emergency boost of energy if required. When a pilot engages afterburner, additional fuel is simply burned in the jetpipe to generate extra thrust. This does consume considerable amounts of fuel and is used sparingly.

At first, jet fighters continued to use the construction techniques and materials employed on piston-engined aircraft. With the dawn of high speed flight and the extreme stresses placed on an airframe, designers began to look beyond aluminium and magnesium alloys and used titanium alloys and specially developed steel. Carbon or graphite fibre composites are also now commonly used and weigh half as much as aluminium alloys but have three times the strength. This major weight saving reduces the overall weight of fighters and allows them to carry more fuel or weaponry if required.

Jet fighter designers have always grappled with the problem of trying to reduce the take-off and landing runs of high speed swept-wing aircraft and thus enable fighters to operate from shorter runways or even sections of road.

A truly innovative solution was the development of swing-wing or variable geometry in which the wings can move automatically from the swept to the spread position to maximize the aircraft's aerodynamic performance as required.

On take-off the spread position generates more lift and gets the aircraft off the ground sooner. Once in the air, the wings can be swept back for high-speed performance. Only a handful of swing-wing fighters have entered service – the F-14 Tomcat, the MiG-23 and the Tornado.

The ultimate solution to the short take-off requirement is the Harrier – the only single-engined vertical or short take-off and landing (V/STOL) aircraft in service. The key to the Harrier's truly remarkable vertical take-off capability lies with the vectored thrust from the Harrier's Rolls-Royce Pegasus engine, directed by four jet nozzles. The nozzles swivel as one, directing thrust from directly to the rear to just forward of vertical. In air combat the nozzles can be used to rapidly decelerate the aircraft so that an enemy aircraft, previously on the Harrier's tail, shoots by, unable to stop, thus becoming the Harrier's prey instead.

Where fighters once had mechanical linkages from control columns to control surfaces, modern fighters have fly-by-wire. This form of electronic signalling eliminates the need for mechanical linkages and a control column – the F-16 for example has a small side stick instead. Computers are now as fundamental to fighters as engines and weapons.

FAR LEFT: **The revolutionary vertical take-off Harrier is equally at home operating from an airfield or a supermarket car park.** INSET LEFT: **The Lockheed F-104 epitomized the quest for better performance.** BELOW: **A Rolls-Royce Spey jet engine. The development of powerplants such as these gave designers the thrust to achieve the required performance.**

Fighter armament

In the years immediately after World War II it became apparent that jet fighters needed better armament than the machine-guns then available, some of which were based on World War I designs. By the end of World War II, Germany was leading the way in fighter armament development and some of their weapons were adopted and improved by the Allies after the war. The highly advanced Mauser MG-213 cannon for example was copied by the USA, Switzerland, France, the Soviet Union and Britain amongst others, and equipped most of the world's air forces in the post-war period. The British version of the Mauser gun, the Aden, is still used today. Even highly evolved cannon have their limitations and cannot for instance be effective over great distances.

The single most important development in aircraft armament since World War II has in fact been the guided Air-to-Air Missile (AAM) with its high explosive warhead. Unguided missiles, many of them developed in World War II, continued to be used into the 1950s. Perhaps the most remarkable of all unguided missiles was the Douglas Genie AAM which to this day is undoubtedly the most devastating of all AAMs. First tested in 1957, the Genie had a 1.5 kiloton nuclear warhead (equivalent to 1500 tons of TNT) with a lethal radius in excess of 305m/1000ft. The launch aircraft's

TOP: **A Royal Air Force Harrier looses off a Sidewinder AAM.** ABOVE: **A Matra Magic II AAM carried by a French Navy Super Etendard.**

on-board computer used radar to track the target and detonated the warhead at the optimum time. Pinpoint accuracy was not necessary with warheads of such destructive power.

Guided air-to-air missiles are now used by fighters to attack enemy aircraft from a minimum of 1.6km/1 mile away and up to distances in excess of 161km/100 miles. Air-to-air missiles

LEFT: **A Tornado F.3 armed with four Sky Flash and two Sidewinder AAMs.** BELOW: **A Royal Air Force F-4 Phantom pictured in 1974 with its armament of SRAAM Sidewinders under the wing, MRAAM Sparrows on the trolley and to the extreme right the pod-mounted 20mm/0.78in Vulcan gun.**

were first used in anger in 1958 when Taiwanese F-86 Sabres clashed with MiG-15s of the People's Republic of China. Armed with early examples of the AIM-9 Sidewinder, the F-86s downed a number of Chinese MiGs with the new weapon.

Modern AAMs are usually infra-red (IR) guided (the missile sensors make it follow a high temperature source such as an engine exhaust) or radar guided (the missile homes in on a target illuminated by a radar from the aircraft, and then follows on its own radar). The latter type normally uses a technique called Semi-Active Radar Homing which allows the radar to operate in pulses, to avoid making itself a target to radar-homing missiles. Some missiles use both the IR and radar guidance methods being radar-guided to within a few miles range and then IR guided to terminate in destruction.

Whatever the guidance, the AAM must reach its target quickly as most only have enough fuel for a few minutes' run. In those missiles with speeds of three or four times the speed of sound, the run can be counted in seconds.

AAMs are usually proximity armed, and, having detected that they are within lethal range, explode rather than having to hit the target. This is to counter last second evasive manoeuvres by the target aircraft and even if a missile just misses the target, the detonation will still cause substantial damage.

Air-to-air missiles are categorized according to their range, into short-range missiles (SRAAMs), medium-range missiles (MRAAMs), and long-range missiles (LRAAMs).

The SRAAM is designed for use in close air combat and distances up to 18km/11 miles and a typical SRAAM would be the well-known and widely used American Sidewinder (AIM-9) series.

The Medium-Range Air-to-Air Missile is mainly used to intercept targets beyond SRAAM range and uses a radar homing system with a greater detection range and better all-weather properties than the infra-red guidance system.

Long-Range Air-to-Air missiles are truly remarkable weapons and perhaps the most impressive of all is the Phoenix carried exclusively by the US Navy F-14 Tomcat. Probably the world's most sophisticated and expensive AAM the Phoenix has a speed of five times the speed of sound, and can be launched from over 200km/124 miles distance from a target, before the F-14 has even appeared on an enemy aircraft radar screen.

With no real alternatives on the horizon, air-to-air missiles will remain the prime armament of fighters for some years to come.

LEFT: **An artist's impression of a Saab Gripen test firing a BVRAAM (Beyond Visual Range Air-to-Air Missile).**

Fighters at war: 1950s–70s

Many fighters developed since the end of World War II have never fired a shot in anger. However, wars have raged around the globe since then, and those that did not directly involve the superpowers often became testing grounds for their equipment. Fighter aircraft have played a key part in most of these conflicts from the Arab-Israeli War to the Falklands, and from the Indian-Pakistan wars to the Gulf War. The performance of these fighters influenced fighter design.

After Korea, the next significant use of fighters came in the 1958 exchanges between Taiwan and the People's Republic of China over disputed territory. In a replay of some of the classic air battles of the Korean War, Taiwanese F-86s took on Chinese MiG-15s. This time the Sabres were armed with air-to-air missiles as well as guns.

India and Pakistan's first air battles took place in 1965. While the Indians deployed the Hawker Hunter, Folland Gnat, Mystère IV and MiG-21, Pakistan had Lockheed F-104s and Sabres which, like the Taiwanese examples, were armed with Sidewinders. Although the Mach 2 F-104 was able to shoot down two Indian Mystères it was shown to be no dogfighter. Indian Hunters were able to outperform enemy Sabres but the F-86 air-to-air missile capability more than evened up the fight.

Fighters entered the fray in Vietnam from 1965 and battled almost constantly until 1973. North Vietnam relied on Soviet equipment including the MiG-17 much favoured by North Vietnam's aces. The MiGs were agile and very dangerous in close combat whereas the USA deployed large, complex missile-armed fighters like the F-4 Phantom designed to hit enemy aircraft from some distance away. The US Navy Crusader, known as the last of the gunfighters, actually achieved 19 out of 20 air victories using AAMs. Despite claims that the dogfight was a thing of the past, Vietnam proved that close air combat expertise was still a vital skill for modern fighter pilots. The US Navy was so concerned with the poor air-combat results from early in the Vietnam War that it set up the now famous Top Gun programme. US Navy pilots were taught how to fight and not just how to fly, and the programme continues to this day.

When the Arab-Israeli War erupted in 1967 the Israelis had Mirage IIIs and, later, the F-4 Phantom, while their Arab opponents flew MiG-19s and MiG-21s. The Mirage III was able to outfly and outgun any aircraft it met in the war and when the F-4 entered Israeli service, the nation had one of the most potent and combat experienced fighter forces in the world. In September 1973 a patrol of Arab MiG-21s attacked a flight of Israeli Mirages and Phantoms off the Syrian coast – 13 MiGs were lost for one Mirage. Fighter aircraft had come a long way since the Korean War but were still only as good as the air fighting system that backed them.

LEFT: **Royal Air Force F-4s. The Phantom saw considerable combat in Vietnam and the Middle East.** TOP AND UPPER MIDDLE: **The MiG-15 (top) and F-86 Sabre (upper middle) had a post-Korea rematch in air battles between Taiwan and the People's Republic of China.** LOWER MIDDLE: **The Hawker Hunter, widely exported from Britain, was used in action by the Indian Air Force during the Indo-Pak war of 1965.** BOTTOM: **The ubiquitous MiG-21.**

Fighters at war: 1980s–90s

Israel's fighter actions against Syria over the Lebanon in 1982 demonstrated how fighters, as part of an integrated strike plan, can win wars. Eighty-two Syrian fighters, mainly MiG-21s and -23s were destroyed without loss by the Israeli fighter force of F-15s and F-16s. Israeli use of all-aspect Sidewinder air-to-air missiles for the first time in combat, allowed their fighters to attack enemy aircraft from any angle and not just the traditional "six o'clock" position to the rear. Ground radar, AWACS and ELINT aircraft all passed information to the Israeli fighters bestowing their pilots with exceptional situational awareness – in short, they knew exactly where the Syrian fighters were and what they were doing.

In 1982 the Falklands War between Britain and Argentina also broke out. Compared to other conflicts, fighter operations over the Falklands were limited but nevertheless absolutely determined the outcome of the war. Fighting a numerically superior enemy, the British pilots had to achieve air superiority over the islands so the ground campaign could begin. British Sea Harriers were tasked with defending the British fleet and

ABOVE: **The swing-wing F-14 Tomcat.** BELOW: **The Mirage 2000, deployed during the Gulf War by France, is an extraordinarily manoeuvrable fighter. Although it has been flying since 1978, the 2000's agility stops the show when it appears at air displays.**

faced the Argentine Mirage IIIs and Daggers. The Argentine fighters, forced to withdraw to the mainland after RAF Vulcan bombing raids on the Port Stanley runway, were operating hundreds of miles from their home bases. In the air combats that took place, British Sea Harriers accounted for 23 enemy aircraft including the very capable Mirages and Israeli-built Daggers – no Sea Harriers were lost in air combat. If the Sea Harriers had not protected the British Task Force so effectively,

ABOVE: **Clearly illustrating the appalling operating conditions in the South Atlantic during the Falklands air war, these Sea Harriers are seen battered by the elements. Nevertheless the Sea Harriers of the Task Force kept the Argentine fighters at bay.** LEFT: **The MiG-21 was widely deployed by a range of air arms in the 1980s and '90s.** BELOW: **The highly capable and potent MiG-29 (this is a German Luftwaffe example) was in the Iraqi Air Force inventory during the Gulf War of 1991.**

Britain's attempt to retake the Falklands could have ended in defeat with the Task Force at the bottom of the South Atlantic.

The rather more one-sided Gulf War of 1991 saw Iraq take on most of the Western world as a result of the invasion of Kuwait. The best fighter in the Iraqi inventory was the Mach 2 plus MiG-29. This very capable, incredibly agile high-performance fighter was developed in the Cold War to take on the best of the West's fighters. With a radar that can track ten targets simultaneously up to 245km/152 miles away, the MiG-29 pilot's helmet-mounted sight allows them to direct air-to-air missiles wherever the pilot looks. Complemented by MiG-21s, -23s, -25s and Mirage F1s, the Iraqi fighter force of MiG-29s was not to be taken lightly. The coalition forces boasted a fighter force of Tornado F.3s, Mirage 2000Cs, F-15Cs, F-16Cs, F-14s and F/A-18s provided by the United States (Air Force, Navy and Marine Corps), Britain (Royal Air Force), Saudi Arabia, France, Qatar and Canada. Although the Iraqi aircraft were very capable in absolute terms, compared to the highly trained coalition pilots backed by the biggest military machine since World War II, Iraqi pilots had little chance of success. The coalition had systematically destroyed the Iraqi military infrastructure piece by piece using bombs and cruise missiles. Despite the massive deployment of coalition fighters only 45 victories were achieved because most Iraqi fighters had fled to safe havens as soon as the shooting began. Without their complex support system, the Iraqi fighters would have been sitting ducks. Thirty-six of the victories were achieved by USAF F-15 Eagles, demonstrating the war-winning ability of the McDonnell Douglas fighter. A further two "kills" were credited to a single Royal Saudi Air Force F-15 that simultaneously shot down two Iraqi Mirage F1s with air-to-air missiles.

The overwhelming weight of coalition fighter power drove the Iraqi Air Force from the sky and allowed the Allied air attacks to continue unopposed. The cease-fire was signed on March 3, 1991 and the fighter had once again helped bring a war to a swift conclusion.

Inflight refuelling

Inflight refuelling (IFR) is vital to the world's major air forces and most recently played a key role in NATO's 1999 air offensive over the Balkans. In the early days of military aviation however, the refuelling of aircraft in flight was seen as nothing more than a stunt and it took some time for the military to be convinced of its value.

In June 1923 the US Army Air Service (USAAS) used two DH4 biplanes to prove a workable, if risky, system consisting of 500 litres/110 gallons of fuel, large funnels, and a 15.25m/ 50ft hose with an "on/off" nozzle on the end. Despite the dangers, by 1935 the record for sustained flight courtesy of inflight refuelling was pushed to 653 hours and 33 minutes – a record that stands to this day.

Although the USA had an early lead it was Britain's Sir Alan Cobham who turned IFR from a stunt to a workable technique. In 1934 Cobham's company Flight Refuelling Ltd developed a system consisting of a weighted cable let out from the tanker and a grapnel fired from the receiving aircraft to grab the cable. The hose was then drawn into the receiver aircraft – it was known as the looped hose system. However, just as World War II was coming to an end, Flight Refuelling perfected a new technique, still in use today – the probe and drogue

TOP: **A Royal Navy Sea Harrier tops up its tanks from a Royal Air Force VC-10 tanker using the probe and drogue technique.** ABOVE: **A USAF "flying boom" prepares to connect to an F-16.**

method. The tanker aircraft trails a hose with a stabilizing conical drogue at its end. Receiving aircraft are fitted with fixed probes which accept fuel flow when connected to the drogue. Valves are automatically opened on the probe and drogue when locked together and shut once contact is broken.

LEFT: **Converted Handley Page Victor bombers served as RAF tankers.**
BELOW: **Tanker operations have been central to fighter operations in a number of conflicts. Here a KC-135 refuels a USAF F4E during the Vietnam War. Two F4Ds (foreground) and two more F4Es (background) await their turn.**

The probe and drogue method was developed and perfected in the late 1940s and was widely adopted, representing a major improvement on the old line and grapnel method. On August 7, 1949 an RAF Meteor Mk 3 was kept airborne for 12 hours and 3 minutes and pilot comfort appeared to be the only limiting factor. In 1951 a specially modified USAF B-29 bomber with three refuelling points became the world's first triple point tanker. In spite of trials in which this B-29 simultaneously kept six RAF Meteor 8s aloft for four hours at a time, the RAF appeared to lose interest in IFR. The triple point tanker was however taken up by the USAF and in the mid-1950s, unlike their British counterparts, all new American fighters were built with IFR probes.

The US Navy also adopted the probe and drogue system in 1954. The Douglas company created the "buddy pack" so that aircraft could carry an air refuelling pod as an external store as easily as a drop tank. This makes for wonderful flexibility as any "buddy-equipped" aircraft can be a tanker or receiver. From the mid-1950s most US Navy and Marine aircraft were also fitted with folding probes.

Meanwhile in the USA, the Boeing company set about developing their own system to improve on the British technique. They wanted to pass fuel at a faster rate down a shorter hose which ultimately evolved into a rigid pipe. So was born the flying boom method used by the USAF today.

The rigid pipe is actually telescopic and joined to the tanker by a universally pivoted coupling. The boom is pressurized by the fuel itself and has aerodynamic control surfaces near the "business" end, controlled by a boom operator or "boomer" who "fires" the telescopic boom to make a fuel-tight seal.

The Boeing KC-135 tanker, developed from the 707 airliner, first flew in August 1956 and swiftly took its place as the tanker aircraft of all time. The KC-135 had a performance that allowed it to fuel thirsty aircraft at jet speed and heights using a high-speed boom transferring 3773 litres/1000 US gallons of fuel per minute. The French Air Force were so impressed by the KC-135 they ordered 12, modified for probe and drogue use, to exclusively refuel the Armée de l'Air Mirage IVA nuclear attack force. In Vietnam, KC-135s transferred almost 3.6 billion kg/8 billion lb of fuel in over 160,000 missions. USAF KC-135s are still in widespread use today and were in the air around the clock during the 1999 NATO action against Serb forces.

During the Gulf War in 1990–1 and the extensive 1999 air campaign against Serb forces, IFR was used throughout both to keep the Allies' aircraft aloft. As long as combat aircraft cannot carry enough fuel to complete lengthy missions, the flying fuel stations of the world's air forces will remain crucial to the plans of aerial warfare strategists.

Pilot equipment in the 21st century

No matter how advanced fighters may become in years to come, as long as there are human pilots they will always need a means of safely abandoning the aircraft in an emergency. One of the most fundamental pieces of pilot equipment is the ejection seat, pioneered during World War II. They are more than just a means of getting pilots and other aircrew out of the aircraft in an emergency – they also have to be comfortable and will be sat on, possibly for thousands of hours without ever being fired. When an ejection seat is fired usually by a handle between the legs or on top of the seat headrest, it draws the occupant's legs in close to the seat with garters (through which the legs are threaded) to keep them from harm's way as the seat rockets from the aircraft. The garters release at the same time as the main harness holding the pilot in the seat is opened.

For a seat to be a true life-saver it must be capable of being fired from ground level and propel itself high enough for the parachute to deploy while not subjecting the pilot to unacceptably dangerous acceleration forces. If a high altitude ejection takes place, modern ejection seats carry their own supply of oxygen so the occupant can breathe easily as soon as ejection has occurred. In reality many aircrew lose their face masks on ejection – some even lose their boots, such can be the violence of an ejection.

When the seat falls below 3050m/10,000ft a barostatic gauge senses the altitude and releases a drogue chute to draw

ABOVE: **Split-second decisions are essential in combat. The Head-Up Display of modern fighters projects vital data on to an angled screen so that the pilot does not waste time constantly looking down at an instrument panel.** LEFT: **A true life-saver – although ejection is a physically traumatic experience, it gives aircrew a means of escape from a striken aircraft at virtually any altitude.**

out the main parachute. Another drogue chute is deployed as soon as the seat leaves the aircraft and slows the seat's descent. All of these functions are automatic in case the occupant is unconscious.

Once clear of the aircraft, the seat automatically releases the occupant from the seat and deploys the main parachute. Although aircrew can suffer injuries due to the rapid acceleration during ejection and the battering they receive as they hit the airflow, possibly at hundreds of miles per hour, they do at least have a means of escape, unlike their 1914 counterparts.

The future?

Cockpit instrumentation has been revolutionized in recent years to relieve the pilot's workload as much as possible so that they can manage the aircraft's systems and fight more effectively.

Helmet-mounted sights have been in use since the mid-1990s but helmet-mounted displays are likely to become the only means of providing the pilot with information. Computers will "clean" the information so that the pilot does not become overloaded with data. A 3-D moving map, painted on the pilot's retina using eye-friendly lasers, will maximize a pilot's situational awareness letting them know exactly where they are in relation to potential enemies.

Pilots are already bombarded with huge volumes of data from on board and other sensors, all of which has to be assimilated by the pilot whilst flying and perhaps fighting.

ABOVE: **Radar equipment carried by today's fighters is far more powerful than that carried during World War II.**

There is however a limit to the amount of information and activities a human can handle simultaneously. Incredibly intelligent software will ultimately be able to provide pilots with instantaneous decision support by assimilating information and recommending an action.

Pilots have relied mainly on sight for flying and fighting whereas systems already under development for the Space Shuttle and the US Navy's Joint Strike Fighter use other senses. Pilots wear a vest bristling with what the manufacturers call "tactors" that vibrate against the pilot's body as a non-visual means of providing information on aircraft orientation. If the aircraft rolls left a tactor vibrates against the pilot's left side and so on.

Complementing visual displays, 3-D audio can also make fuller use of the pilot's senses – a left engine failure for

TOP: **The Eurofighter cockpit is dominated by a wide-angle Head-Up Display and three colour monitors displaying all instrument information and flight data. The pilot has a helmet-mounted sight for weapon aiming and direct voice input allows the pilot to control certain aspects of the flight just by talking to the aircraft.** ABOVE: **Helmet-mounted sights were introduced in the mid-1990s.**

example could be signalled to the pilot via an audible tone in the left ear.

Some experts are claiming, not for the first time in the history of fighter aircraft, that the days of the manned fighter may be coming to an end. Time will tell, but for the foreseeable future, air combat will be fought with humans in the cockpit.

A–Z of Modern Fighter Aircraft

1945 to the Present Day

By the end of World War II, piston-engined fighters had been developed as far as they could go. Although many remained in service for some years, jet fighters were clearly the way ahead and effectively rendered the piston fighter obsolete. After limited use towards the end of World War II, jets were within a decade regularly flying at supersonic speeds, if only in dives. Wartime German aerodynamic research and experiments revolutionized post-war fighter design, and as swept-wing fighters began to appear, supersonic flight became routine. Many of the fighters featured in the following pages were conceived in the Cold War to tackle fleets of enemy bombers carrying deadly nuclear cargoes. These sophisticated fighters were sometimes bigger than World War II bombers and weighed more than 20 times as much as World War I fighters. Some were never used in anger, possibly serving to deter their enemy from attack, while others have been used many times in conventional wars around the globe.

New ideas for fighter configurations, new materials and construction techniques, and even more complex on-board systems will shape the fighter aircraft of the future.

LEFT: **Lockheed P-80A Shooting Star, the first US jet fighter in military service.**

LEFT: **The US design influence on the Ching-kuo is clear in this photograph.**

AIDC Ching-kuo

First flight: May 28, 1989
Power: Two International Turbofan Engine Company 4269kg/9400lb afterburning-thrust TFE1042-70 turbofans
Armament: One 20mm/0.78in cannon, plus six hardpoints for a variety of AAMs, anti-ship missiles and bombs
Size: Wingspan – 8.53m/28ft
Length – 13.26m/43ft 6in
Height – 4.65m/15ft 3in
Wing area – 24.3m²/261.1sq ft
Weights: Empty – 6485kg/14,300lb
Maximum take-off – 12,245kg/27,000lb
Performance: Maximum speed – 1295kph/804mph
Ceiling – 16,470m/54,000ft
Range – Approx. 965km/600 miles
Climb – 15,250m/50,000ft per minute

AIDC Ching-kuo

Also known as the Indigenous Defensive Fighter (IDF), the Ching-kuo (named after the late President Chiang Ching-kuo) was built in Taiwan with major technical help from US companies, notably General Dynamics. The aircraft bears more than a passing resemblance to the F-16 and is essentially a smaller version of the famous General Dynamics fighter. Development began after a 1982 arms embargo by the USA was imposed (to improve relations with China), prohibiting the import by Taiwan of US fighter aircraft. It did not however prohibit technical help, which is why the Ching-kuo is an F-20A Tigershark nose married to the body, wings and fin of an F-16.

Taiwan wanted the IDF to replace ageing F-5 and F-104 Starfighter fighters – the IDF accelerates faster than the F-104 and can turn inside an F-5. The prototype first flew in May 1989, deliveries to the Republic of China Air Force began in January 1994 and the last of 130 examples was delivered in January 2000.

Armstrong Whitworth Meteor nightfighters

LEFT: **The NF.11 was the first Meteor nightfighter, and was built until 1954.**

Armstrong Whitworth Meteor NF.11

First flight: May 31, 1950
Power: Two Rolls-Royce 1588kg/3500lb static-thrust Derwent 8 turbojet engines
Armament: Four 20mm/0.78in cannon mounted in wings
Size: Wingspan – 13.11m/43ft
Length – 14.78m/48ft 6in Height – 4.24m/13ft 11in
Wing area – 34.75m²/374sq ft
Weights: Empty – 5451kg/12,091lb
Maximum take-off – 9088kg/20,035lb
Performance: Maximum speed – 933kph/580mph
Ceiling – 12,192m/40,000ft
Range – 1480km/920 miles
Climb – 9144m/30,000ft in 11 minutes, 12 seconds

Wartime Mosquitos were Britain's nightfighter defence from the end of the war until Meteor (and Vampire) nightfighters entered service in 1951.

The Meteor NF.11 was built as a stop-gap while delays of the all-weather Javelin dragged on. The NF.11 was basically a Meteor Mk 7 trainer with the new AI Mk 10 radar in an enlarged nose. The rear cockpit's dual-controls were replaced by navigator/radar operator equipment and displays. Cannon were moved from the nose out to the long span wing. The Meteor 8's tail completed the composite nightfighter which first flew in May 1950. Derwent 8s were the chosen powerplant and 335 NF.11s were produced up to 1954. The tropicalized version of the Mk 11 was the Mk 13, 40 of which were built – they only served with two RAF units in the Middle East and six were later sold on to Egypt.

The Mk 12 had improved American APS-21 radar and first flew in April 1953 powered by Derwent 9s – altogether 97 of these were built.

The Meteor NF.14 was the last of the line and can be identified by its clear vision two-piece canopy – the aircraft was also some 43.2cm/17in longer than previous NF marks. It was an NF.14 of No.60 Squadron in Singapore that flew the RAF's last Meteor sortie in 1961.

Armstrong Whitworth built a total of 547 Meteor nightfighters.

Armstrong Whitworth (Hawker) Sea Hawk

The Sea Hawk is remarkable for two reasons – it was the first standard jet fighter of Britain's Fleet Air Arm and it remained in front-line service long after swept-wing fighters equipped navies elsewhere. Also, the aircraft's layout was unusual in that the single jet engine jet pipe was bifurcated (split) to feed two exhaust ducts, one at each trailing-edge wing root. The leading-edge wing roots incorporated the two corresponding air intakes.

The first incarnation of the Sea Hawk was the Hawker P.1040, which flew in September 1947 and was proposed as a new fighter for both the Royal Navy and the RAF. Only the Navy placed orders for the Sea Hawk and after building just 35 production Sea Hawk fighters, Hawkers transferred production to Armstrong Whitworth, hence the

occasional confusion over the Sea Hawk manufacturer's identity. As a design the Sea Hawk certainly looked right, coming from the same team that designed the Hurricane and, later, the Hunter.

The first Royal Navy Sea Hawk squadron, No.806, formed in March 1953, carrying its distinctive ace of diamonds logo on its Sea Hawk Mk 1s. In February the following year, 806 embarked on HMS *Eagle*. The most widely-used Sea Hawk version was the Mk 3 fighter-bomber, capable of carrying considerable amounts of ordnance under its wings. This change in usage was due to the realization that the Sea Hawk's performance could not match that of potential enemies in air-to-air combat. That said, the Fleet Air Arm's Sea Hawks did see action in the ground-attack role during the 1956 Suez Crisis, with Sea Venoms as fighter escort. The type continued in front-line FAA service until 1960, but some continued in second-line roles until 1969.

Some ex-Royal Navy aircraft were supplied to the Royal Australian and Canadian navies but the biggest export customers were the West German naval air arm, Holland and the Indian Navy.

ABOVE: **The Sea Hawk was the Royal Navy's first standard jet fighter.** LEFT: **Fleet Air Arm Sea Hawks saw action during the Suez Crisis of 1956.**

Dutch aircraft were equipped to carry an early version of the Sidewinder air-to-air missile until their phasing-out in 1964. German Sea Hawks operated exclusively from land bases in the air defence role until the mid-1960s. The Indian Navy's Sea Hawks saw action in the war with Pakistan in 1971 and continued to be flown, remarkably, into the mid-1980s, when they were replaced by Sea Harriers.

Armstrong Whitworth (Hawker) Sea Hawk F. Mk 1

First flight: September 2, 1947 (P.1040)
Power: Rolls-Royce 2268kg/5000lb thrust Nene 101 turbojet
Armament: Four 20mm/0.78in Hispano cannon beneath cockpit floor
Size: Wingspan – 11.89m/39ft
Length – 12.08m/39ft 8in
Height – 2.79m/8ft 8in
Wing area – 25.83m²/278sq ft
Weights: Empty – 4173kg/9200lb
Maximum take-off – 7355kg/16,200lb
Performance: Maximum speed – 901kph/560mph
Ceiling – 13,176m/43,200ft
Range – 1191km/740 miles
Climb – 10,675m/35,000ft in 12 minutes, 5 seconds

Atlas/Denel Cheetah

The multi-role Cheetah was developed in response to a 1977 United Nations arms embargo against South Africa. At the time, the South Africans were hoping to import combat aircraft to replace their ageing 1960s Mirage IIIs but instead looked to develop and improve the existing airframes. State-owned Atlas already had experience of assembling imported Mirage F1 kits. Arguably the most comprehensive upgrade of the Mirage III achieved anywhere, the result was one of the world's most capable combat aircraft. Though never officially disclosed, the updates were undertaken with the assistance of IAI of Israel who had upgraded their own Mirages to Kfir standard.

Nearly 50 per cent of the airframe was replaced, canard foreplanes, new avionics and weapons systems were added, and more powerful engines were installed in two-seaters.

The first Cheetah unveiled in 1986 was the Cheetah D attack aircraft, a two-seat upgraded version of the Mirage IIIDZ two-seater. Single-seat Cheetah fighters, declared operational in 1987, were designated EZ and kept the old Mirage SNECMA Atar 9C engine but this version led to the Cheetah C fighter, considered by many to be the ultimate Mirage upgrade. Developed in great secrecy, news of the C model only reached the outside world in the early 1995. With a powerful radar, state-of-the-art cockpit avionics and advanced self-defence systems, the Cheetah C's main armament is indigenous South African air-to-air missiles.

TOP: **The Cheetah is one of the world's most capable combat aircraft.** ABOVE: **The two-seat attack D version was developed from the Mirage IIIDZ.** BELOW: **The Cheetah is the ultimate Mirage III development.**

Atlas/Denel Cheetah EZ

First flight: Believed to be 1986
Power: SNECMA 6209kg/13,670lb thrust Atar 9C turbojet
Armament: One 30mm/1.18in cannon plus V3B Kukri, V3C Darter, Python and Shafrir air-to-air missiles as well as bombs/rockets
Size: Wingspan – 8.22m/26ft 11in
Length – 15.5m/51ft
Height – 4.5m/14ft 9in
Wing area – 34.8m^2/374.6sq ft
Weights: Empty – 6608kg/14,550lb
Maximum take-off – 13,700kg/30,200lb
Performance: Maximum speed – 2338kph/1452mph
Ceiling – 17,000m/55,777ft
Range and climb data are not published but likely to be similar to Mirage IIIE, i.e. 1200km/745 miles and 7930m/26,000ft in 3 minutes

Avro Canada CF-100 Canuck

The CF-100 was the first combat aircraft of indigenous Canadian design and had its maiden flight in January 1950. This large and impressive interceptor was designed very quickly for the Royal Canadian Air Force (RCAF) to operate at night, in all weathers and with great range to protect the vast expanses of Canadian airspace.

The first true fighter version, the Mk 3, entered RCAF service in 1952, armed with eight machine-guns housed in a "belly" pack beneath the rear cockpit. The Mk 4 had a more powerful engine and was armed with wingtip pods, each containing 29 Mighty Mouse air-to-air rockets that could be fired by an on-board computer. Having steered the aircraft on a collision course with

the target using the radar housed in the nose, the computer could then fire the rockets at the optimum range. Additional rockets or guns could be carried in the belly.

In 1957 the joint Canadian/US North American Air Defense Command (NORAD) was established and the RCAF Canucks joined the USAF F-86s, F-89s and F-94s, ranged to protect North America against Soviet incursion from the north. The Canuck's short take-off run allowed it to fly from small airstrips and its good climb rate meant it could reach incoming Soviet aircraft very quickly if needed.

The ultimate CF-100, the Mk 5, had even more powerful engines and a 1.83m/6ft increase in wingspan for better high-altitude performance. Fifty-three of this final version were also supplied to Belgium, where they comprised the 1st All-Weather Interception Wing. These excellent and underrated fighters protected Canadian skies through to 1981.

ABOVE: **A Mk 4B of No.445 Squadron, Royal Canadian Air Force.** LEFT: **The underrated CF-100 was a key Cold War fighter.** BELOW: **This Mk 4 is preserved in the UK by the Imperial War Museum at Duxford.**

Avro Canada CF-100 Canuck Mk 5

First flight: January 19, 1950
Power: Two Orenda 14 3300kg/7275lb thrust turbojets
Armament: 58 Mighty Mouse 70mm/2.75in unguided air-to-air rockets, carried in two wingtip pods, 29 in each
Size: Wingspan – 17.7m/58ft
  Length – 16.5m/54ft 1in
  Height – 4.72m/15ft 7in
  Wing area – 54.8m²/591sq ft
Weights: Empty – 10,478kg/23,100lb
  Maximum take-off – 16,783kg/37,000lb
Performance: Maximum speed – 1046kph/650mph
  Ceiling – 16,460m/54,000ft
  Range – 1046km/650 miles
  Climb – 9144m/30,000ft in 5 minutes

BAE Systems Harrier/Sea Harrier

The Harrier is among the best examples of British innovation in the field of aircraft design. This truly remarkable aircraft, constantly improved and updated since its first hovering flight in October 1960, is still the only single-engined vertical or short take-off and landing (V/STOL) in service. It enables military planners to wield air power without the need for airfields.

During the Cold War it was obvious that the West's military airfields would have been attacked very early in any offensive. Dispersal of aircraft and equipment was one option of response – the other was the Harrier, with its ability to operate from any small piece of flat ground. The Harrier is equally at home operating from a supermarket car park or woodland clearing as it is from conventional airfields. The fact that an aircraft can take off vertically with no need for forward movement still leaves spectators stunned over four decades after the prototype carried out its first uncertain and tethered hover.

The Harrier can take off and land vertically by the pilot selecting an 80-degree nozzle angle and applying full power. At 15–30m/50–100ft altitude, the nozzles are gradually directed

ABOVE: **Two Royal Navy Sea Harrier FRS. Mk 1s. Developed from the land-based Harrier, the naval versions of the type have been a great success.** LEFT: **Although it has an air-to-air combat facility, the Harrier GR.7 is a versatile all-weather ground-attack aircraft.**

rearwards until conventional wingborne flight is achieved. The key to the Harrier's vertical take-off lies with the vectored thrust from the aircraft's Pegasus engine, directed by four jet nozzles controlled by a selector lever next to the throttle in the cockpit. The nozzles swivel as one, directing thrust from directly to the rear to just forward of vertical. While hovering or flying at very low speeds, the aircraft is controlled in all planes of movement by reaction control jets located in the nose, wing and tail. These jets are operated by the Harrier's conventional rudder pedals and control column.

The Harrier's agility is legendary and it is able to make very tight turns by using the nozzles. In air combat the nozzles can be used to decelerate the aircraft rapidly so that an enemy aircraft, previously on the Harrier's tail, shoots by, unable to stop – it becomes the Harrier's prey instead.

The Harrier GR.1 first entered squadron service with the RAF in October 1969 and many were subsequently upgraded to GR.3 standard, with more powerful engines and a tail warning radar to alert pilots to hostile missiles locking on to their aircraft. Early in the Harrier's operational life, the US Marine Corps expressed an interest in the aircraft, leading to more than a hundred being built as the AV-8A by McDonnell Douglas in the USA. The USMC continue to operate Harriers today with the AV-8B variant, which is roughly equivalent to the GR.7 in current RAF service. The other customer for the early Harrier was the Spanish Navy, who ordered the US-built AV-8A and who subsequently sold some of the aircraft on to the Thai Navy in 1996. Manufacture of new AV-8Bs and GR.7s stopped in late 1997, when AV-8Bs were supplied to the Italian Navy. Many existing aircraft are, however, being upgraded to Harrier II Plus standard, allowing the Harrier to carry more weaponry over a greater distance. Improved radar and compatibility with the AMRAAM air-to-air missile can be part of the upgrade.

ABOVE: **Sea Harrier FA.2s pictured on the deck of Britain's HMS *Illustrious* in 1995.** LEFT: **The Harrier can provide versatile and flexible air power from small unexpected locations.**

The Harrier's V/STOL capability was not lost on naval strategists and in February 1963 an early version of the Harrier landed on HMS *Ark Royal* at sea. The Royal Navy ordered a maritime version in 1975 and the Sea Harrier FRS. Mk 1 flew for the first time in August 1978. This aircraft was similar to the GR.3 but had a completely redesigned front fuselage, different avionics and was powered by a special version of the Pegasus engine (104), with improved corrosion resistance. Examples of this version were exported to the Indian Navy as FRS.51s. The Sea Harriers are true fighter aircraft, while the Harriers are close air support aircraft.

The Sea Harrier FA.2 was a mid-life upgrade of the FRS.1, with changes to the airframe, armament, avionics, radar and cockpit. The FA.2 was the first European fighter to be equipped with the AIM-120 AMRAAM air-to-air missile. The Royal Navy's FA.2s made their combat début in August 1994 over Bosnia, operated by No.899 Squadron from the deck of HMS *Invincible*. Early versions of the Sea Harrier, however, had already been in action with the FAA 12 years earlier. In 1982 Britain's Task Force sailed south on its 12,872km/8000 mile journey to retake the Falkland Islands but it faced serious opposition from Argentine forces. Against considerable odds, the combined Harrier force of RAF and Fleet Air Arm pilots and machines flew a total of 1850 missions and destroyed 32 Argentine aircraft, 23 of them in air combat, including high-performance Daggers.

Two-seat trainer versions of all marks have been produced.

ABOVE: **Harriers are still flying more than 40 years after the prototype first took to the sky.** BELOW LEFT: **The distinctive nose of the FA.2 houses the advanced Blue Vixen radar.**

BAE Systems Sea Harrier FA.2

First flight: September 19, 1988

Power: Rolls-Royce 9765kg/21,500lb-thrust Pegasus 106 turbofan

Armament: Four AIM-120 air-to-air missiles or two AIM-120s and four AIM-9 Sidewinders. Two 30mm/1.18in Aden cannon can also be carried on underfuselage stations, as well as up to 2270kg/5000lb of bombs, rockets and anti-ship missiles

Size: Wingspan – 7.7m/25ft 3in
Length – 14.17m/46ft 6in
Height – 3.71m/12ft 2in
Wing area – 18.7m^2/201sq ft

Weights: Empty – 6374kg/14,052lb
Maximum take-off – 11,880kg/26,200lb

Performance Maximum speed – 1185kph/736mph
Ceiling – 15,555m/51,000ft
Range – 1300km/800 miles
Climb – 15,240m/50,000ft per minute at VTOL weight

McDonnell Douglas/Boeing F-15

The F-15 Eagle, designed to succeed the legendary F-4 Phantom, is an all-weather, highly manoeuvrable fighter originally designed to gain and maintain US Air Force air superiority in aerial combat. It is probably the most capable multi-role fighter in service today. Between entering service in 1974 and 2000, the F-15 has achieved an unprecedented air combat record with 100.5 victories for zero losses.

The first F-15A flight was made in July 1972, and the first flight of the two-seat F-15B trainer followed in July 1973. The first USAF Eagle (an F-15B) was delivered to the Air Force in November 1974. The first Eagle destined for a front-line combat squadron was delivered in January 1976, and some squadrons were combat-ready by the end of the year.

The Eagle's air superiority is achieved through a mixture of incredible manoeuvrability and acceleration, range, weapons and avionics. It can penetrate enemy defence and outperform and outfight any current enemy aircraft. The F-15 has electronic systems and weaponry to detect, acquire, track and attack enemy aircraft while operating in friendly or enemy-controlled airspace. The weapons and flight control systems are designed so one person can safely and effectively perform air-to-air combat.

The F-15's superior manoeuvrability and acceleration are achieved through high engine thrust-to-weight ratio and low wing loading. Low wing loading (the ratio of aircraft weight to its wing area) is a vital factor in manoeuvrability and, combined with the high thrust-to-weight ratio, enables the aircraft to turn tightly without losing airspeed.

The F-15's avionics system sets it apart from other fighter aircraft. It includes a Head-Up Display, advanced radar, ultra-high frequency communications, and an instrument landing system for automatic landings. The Eagle also has an internally mounted, tactical electronic-warfare system, "identification friend or foe" system, electronic countermeasures set and a central digital computer system.

The Head-Up Display projects on the windscreen all essential flight information gathered by the integrated avionics system. This display, visible in any light condition, provides the pilot with information necessary to track and destroy an enemy aircraft without having to look down at cockpit instruments.

ABOVE: **An F-15E – this two-seat Strike Eagle was based in the UK at RAF Lakenheath.** BELOW: **The F-15 is a world-class fighter with a remarkable combat record. The USAF will operate F-15s for some years to come.**

LEFT: **Widely deployed in Europe during the Cold War, the F-15 actually first saw combat in Israeli service in 1977.** BELOW: **F-15As of the 21st Tactical Fighter Wing based at Elmendorf AFB, Alaska, helped protect North America from an attack over the North Pole.**

The F-15's versatile pulse-Doppler radar can look up at high-flying targets and down at low-flying targets, detect and track aircraft and small high-speed targets at distances beyond visual range down to close range and at altitudes down to treetop level. The radar feeds target information into the central computer for effective weapons delivery. For close-in dogfights, the radar automatically acquires enemy aircraft, and this information is projected on the Head-Up Display. The F-15's electronic warfare system provides both threat warning and automatic countermeasures against selected threats.

The single-seat F-15C and two-seat F-15D models entered the USAF inventory from 1979. Among the improvements were 900kg/2000lb of additional internal fuel and provision for "conformal" fuel tanks that fit flush with the fuselage.

The F-15E Strike Eagle, first flight July 1980, is a two-seat, dual-role fighter for all-weather, air-to-air and deep interdiction missions – the rear cockpit is reserved for the weapons systems officer. It can fight its way to a target over long ranges, destroy ground targets and fight its way out. Its engines incorporate advanced digital technology for improved-performance acceleration – from a standstill to maximum afterburner takes less than four seconds.

The F-15's combat début came not with the USAF but with export customer Israel who shot down four Syrian MiG-21s in June 1977. Unconfirmed numbers of Syrian fighters were also shot down by Israeli F-15s in 1982. USAF F-15C, D and E models were in action during the Gulf War where they proved their superior combat capability with a confirmed 36 air-to-air victories. Saudi F-15s also downed Iraqi aircraft in combat. In the 1999 Balkans conflict, USAF F-15s destroyed four Serb MiG-29s.

More than 1500 F-15s have been produced for the USA and international customers Israel, Japan and Saudi Arabia. The F-15I Thunder, a model designed for Israel, has been built in the USA, the first of 25 Thunders arriving in Israel in January 1998.

LEFT: **F-15s proved their worth during the Gulf War. Here a Royal Saudi Air Force F-15C is seen refuelling from a USAF tanker.**

McDonnell Douglas F-15A

First flight: July 27, 1972

Power: Two Pratt & Whitney 11340kg/25000lb afterburning thrust F100-PW-100 turbofans

Armament: One 20mm/0.78in cannon, four AIM-7 Sparrow and four AIM-9 Sidewinder AAMs plus up to 7267kg/16,000lb of other weaponry on five hardpoints

Size: Wingspan – 13.04m/42ft 9.5in
Length – 19.44m/63ft 9.5in
Height – 5.64m/18ft 6in
Wing area – 56.48m^2/608sq ft

Weights: Empty – 12,247kg/27,000lb
Maximum take-off – 25,402kg/56,000lb

Performance: Maximum speed – 2655kph/1650mph
Ceiling – 19,200m/63,000ft
Range – 966km/600 miles
Climb – 15,250m/50,000ft per minute

Boeing/McDonnell Douglas/Northrop F/A-18 Hornet

The twin-engine Hornet was developed for the US Navy from the YF-17 project that Northrop had proposed for the US Air Force. As the company had no experience building carrier-borne aircraft, it teamed up with McDonnell Douglas (now Boeing) to develop the F-17. Two versions, ground attack and fighter, were originally proposed but the two roles were combined in the very capable F/A-18, the first of which flew in 1978. With its excellent fighter and self-defence capabilities,

the F/A-18 was intended to increase strike mission survivability and supplement the F-14 Tomcat in US Navy fleet air defence.

The F/A-18's advanced radar and avionics systems allow its pilots to shift from fighter to strike mode on the same mission by the flip of a switch, a facility used routinely by Hornets in Operation Desert Storm in 1991 – they fought their way to a target by defeating opposing aircraft and then attacking ground targets. This "force multiplier" capability gives more flexibility in employing tactical aircraft in a rapidly changing battle scenario.

ABOVE: **The remarkable F/A-18 is, at the flip of a switch, a fighter or a strike aircraft. The type was proven in combat during the Gulf War.** LEFT: **The Hornet was originally intended to support the F-14 in defending the US Fleet in the air.**

In addition to air superiority, fighter escort and forward air control missions, the F/A-18 is equally capable in the air-defence suppression, reconnaissance, close air support and strike mission roles. Designed to be reliable and easily maintainable, survivability was another key consideration and was proven by taking direct hits from surface-to-air missiles, recovering successfully, being repaired quickly and flying again the next day.

The F/A-18 Hornet was built in single- and two-seat versions. Although the two-seater is a conversion trainer, it is also combat capable and has a surprisingly similar performance to the single-seat version although with reduced range. The F/A-18A and C are single-seat aircraft while the F/A-18B and D are two-seaters. The B model is used primarily for training, while the D model is the current US Navy aircraft for attack, tactical air control, forward air control and reconnaissance squadrons.

In November 1989, the first F/A-18s equipped with night strike capability were delivered, and since 1991 F/A-18s have been delivered with F404-GE-402 enhanced-performance engines that produce up to 20 per cent more thrust than the previous F404 engines. From May 1994, the Hornet has been equipped with upgraded radar – the APG-73, which substantially increases the speed and memory capacity of the radar's processors. These upgrades and improvements help the Hornet maintain its advantage over potential enemies and keep it among the most advanced and capable combat aircraft in the world.

Apart from the US Navy and Marine Corps, the F/A-18 is also in service with the air forces of Canada, Australia, Spain, Kuwait, Finland, Switzerland and Malaysia.

Canada was the first international customer for the F/A-18, and its fleet of 138 CF-18 Hornets is the largest outside the United States. The CF-18s have an unusual element to their paint scheme in that a "fake" cockpit is painted on the underside of the fuselage directly beneath the real cockpit. This is intended to confuse an enemy fighter, if only for a split second, about the orientation of the CF-18 in close air combat. That moment's hesitation can mean the difference between kill or be killed in a dogfight situation.

ABOVE: **The twin fins canted at 30 degrees are a prime recognition feature of the F/A-18.** LEFT: **A US Marine Corps F/A-18D. This versatile version is equipped for improved weapons delivery and has better radar and more effective armament.**

The manufacturers have devised a life extension programme that will keep the Hornet in the front line until 2019.

The F/A-18E/F Super Hornet was devised to build on the great success of the Hornet and, having been test flown in November 1995, entered service for evaluation with US Navy squadron VFA-122 in November 1999. It was approved for US Navy service and the first Super Hornet fleet deployment was scheduled for 2002. Export versions were expected to be available in 2005. The Super Hornet is 25 per cent larger than its predecessor but has 42 per cent fewer parts. Both the single-seat E and two-seat F models offer increased range, greater endurance, more payload-carrying ability and more powerful engines in the form of the F414-GE-400, an advanced derivative of the Hornet's current F404 engine family that produces 35 per cent more thrust.

Structural changes to the airframe increase internal fuel capacity by 1633kg/3600lb which extends the Hornet's mission radius by up to 40 per cent. The fuselage is 86.3cm/ 34in longer and the wing is 25 per cent larger with an extra 9.3m²/100sq ft of surface area. There are two additional weapons stations, bringing the total to 11.

In the words of its manufacturers "The Super Hornet is an adverse-weather, day and night, multi-mission strike fighter whose survivability improvements over its predecessors make it harder to find, and if found, harder to hit, and if hit, harder to disable".

ABOVE: **US Marine Corps F/A-18 Hornets of VFA-25, pictured on the deck of USS** *Independence* **in 1991.**

Boeing/McDonnell Douglas/Northrop F/A-18C Hornet

First flight: November 18, 1978

Power: Two General Electric 7267kg/16,000lb thrust F404-GE-400 turbofans

Armament: One 20mm/0.78in cannon, nine hard points carrying up to 7031kg/15,500lb of weapons including AIM-7, AIM-120 AMRAAM, AIM-9 air-to-air missiles or other guided weapons, bombs and rockets

Size: Wingspan – 11.43m/37ft 6in
Length – 17.07m/56ft
Height – 4.66m/15ft 3in
Wing area – 37.2m²/400sq ft

Weights: Empty – 10,455kg/23,050lb
Maximum take-off – 25,400kg/56,000lb

Performance: Maximum speed – 1915kph/1189mph
Ceiling – 15,250m/50,000ft
Range – 3336km/2027 miles
Climb – 13,725m/45,000ft per minute

British Aircraft Corporation/English Electric Lightning

When the very high-performance Lightning joined front-line squadrons in 1960, it gave the RAF an interceptor capable of a performance way beyond any of its predecessors. During a lengthy development and testing programme, the Lightning became the first aircraft to exceed the speed of sound in level flight over the UK. With a top speed of around 2.5 times the speed of sound and a climb rate that few fighters have ever equalled, the Lightning was the fastest British fighter ever.

Design work for the aircraft began in 1947, when English Electric were awarded a study contract for a supersonic research aircraft. Extensive research into swept-wing fighters had been carried out in German wind tunnels during World War II, and the English Electric designers looked carefully at the data. The fruit of the study was the P.1A, which first flew in August 1954 and soon exceeded Mach 1, the speed of sound. The aerodynamics of the aircraft were considered to be so complex that Britain's first transonic wind tunnel was constructed to help with development. A scaled-down flying test bed was also built by Short Brothers to test the various swept-wing and tailplane configurations.

ABOVE: **XS897, a Lightning F.6 of No.56 Squadron, pictured in 1975. Note the phoenix and flames unit badge on the tail and the 1930s era chequerboard design by the roundel.** BELOW: **Range was always an issue with the Lightning – this F.3 has overwing ferry tanks as well as a large ventral fuel tank.**

The design was eventually refined and became the P.1B, powered by Avon turbojets, the two engines mounted one above the other with the nose acting as one large air intake. In November 1958, fitted with afterburning Avons, the P.1B topped Mach 2 for the first time. The Lightning, as it was then

LEFT: **Demonstrating the Lightning's unusual outboard retraction of the undercarriage, this aircraft has its burners lit and is preparing to go vertical.** BELOW: **This F.6, XS928, was based at RAF Binbrook for the last years of its RAF service.** BOTTOM: **The Lightning was the last all-British-built fighter in RAF service.**

called, was cleared for service shortly afterwards. The first RAF unit to receive the new Lightning was No.74 Squadron, based at Coltishall.

The Lightning was a relatively complicated aircraft compared to its predecessors, but it did give the RAF an all-weather fighter that could have held its own with any other fighters of the time. The radar, housed in the cone at the entrance to the air intake, could search above and below the horizon, take the aircraft to within firing range of a target and then automatically loose off two Firestreak or Red Top air-to-air missiles. Thus the Lightning was the RAF's first single-seat fighter integrated weapons system, as opposed to a simple gun platform.

Modifications to the Lightning throughout its service life improved its performance and it remained a viable air defence weapon until its retirement. When the F. Mk 1A was introduced it included an inflight refuelling capability, giving the Lightning the ability to transit over long distances such as the North Sea. The Lightning Mk 6 had a new wing that improved the aircraft's performance to the point where the fuel load could be doubled without significantly affecting performance.

A two-seat version, the T. Mk 5, was developed as a trainer and first flew in March 1962, accommodating the instructor and pupil side by side with duplicated instruments and controls. The change to the forward fuselage profile did nothing to slow the version down, as it was still capable of achieving Mach 2.3. Tornado F.3s finally replaced the last RAF Lightnings in 1988.

Saudi Arabia and Kuwait both operated export versions of the F. Mk 6, which served in the multi-role fighter and ground-attack roles. In 1969, Saudi Lightning F.53s flew ground-attack missions against targets in Yemen.

The Lightning was the last solely UK-designed fighter to enter RAF service and is considered by many to be the peak of UK fighter development.

BAC Lightning F. Mk 6

First flight: April 4, 1957 (P.1B)
Power: Two Rolls-Royce 7420kg/16,360lb-thrust Avon 301 afterburning turbojets
Armament: Two Red Top or Firestreak infra-red homing air-to-air missiles or two batteries of 22 50mm/2in unguided rockets. Twin 30mm/1.18in Aden cannon can also be carried in a ventral pack
Size: Wingspan – 10.62m/34ft 10in
Length – 16.84m/55ft 3in, including probe
Height – 5.97m/19ft 7in
Wing area – 42.97m^2/458.5sq ft
Weights: Empty – 12,717kg/28,041lb
Maximum take-off – 19,047kg/42,000lb
Performance: Maximum speed – 2112kph/1320mph
Ceiling – 16,770m/55,000ft
Range – 1290km/800 miles
Climb – 15,240m/50,000ft per minute

Convair F-102 Delta Dagger

In 1950 the US Air Force invited designs for a fighter that could exceed the performance of known Soviet bombers, but this aircraft would be ground-breaking because it was going to be just one part of a weapon package built around the Hughes Electronic Control System. The successful proposal came from Convair and led to the first fighter to be developed as part of an integrated weapons system, the F-102, and ultimately the F-106. Convair's design had an unorthodox delta (triangular) wing, which was, it turned out, a little ahead of its time. The company had some experience of deltas already, having produced the experimental XF-92 research aircraft inspired by the German wartime deltas of Dr Alexander Lippisch.

Development delays with the proposed Wright J67 engine and the various electronic "black boxes" forced the USAF to ask Convair to develop an interim version of the proposed new fighter, which was then designated F-102. The original design progressed to become the F-106. Far from being a spin-off or a poor relation, the F-102 became a very able combat aircraft and was the first fighter armed only with missiles, the AIM-4 and AIM-26 Falcon.

The F-102's development was far from painless – during its maiden flight in October 1953 it became apparent that the aircraft was incapable of exceeding the speed of sound in level flight, which had been a basic requirement from the USAF.

The design team had literally to go back to the drawing board to overcome the high levels of transonic drag. The fuselage was lengthened by 1.21m/4ft, the air intakes and the fin were made bigger and the wing was modified too. By then the Pratt and Whitney J57 engine had been chosen, to help the aircraft

TOP: **The F-102 came about as an interim version of the F-106 but was a potent fighter in its own right.**

ABOVE: **A total of 875 F-102s were delivered to the US Air Force.**

punch through the sound barrier. Test flights beginning in December 1954 showed the modifications had worked and the design could indeed fly faster than Mach 1. The first production version flew in June 1955, and the F-102 finally entered USAF service in April 1956, three years later than planned. In doing so it became the first supersonic delta-winged aircraft to reach operational status.

By 1958, 26 squadrons of F-102s equipped the USAF's Air Defense Command but this was the peak. The 102 was always seen as an interim aircraft by the USAF, plugging the gap while the F-106 was developed. The F-102 did, however, continue in the front line with the USAF in Europe, Alaska and the Pacific for some years and was the main fighter equipment of the Air National Guard through to the early 1970s. The last Air Defense Command unit to operate the F-102 was the 57th Fighter Interception Squadron, based at Keflavik in Iceland, who finally relinquished their machines in April 1973.

In the F-102 cockpit the pilot had two control columns to handle – one managed the aircraft's movements, while the other was used to control the impressive on-board radar, which could pick up an enemy aircraft and direct the aircraft to the target. Pilots then had to choose their weapons from between small unguided rockets, carried within the doors of the weapons bay, or Falcon air-to-air missiles, one of which could have been nuclear-tipped. The Falcons were stored in the aircraft's internal weapons bay until the pilot or the fire control system extended them for firing.

Exported models of ex-USAF Delta Daggers were supplied to the air forces of Greece and Turkey in the early 1970s. Around 200 ex-USAF F-102s also became pilotless target aircraft, helping the USAF's "top guns" perfect their weapon skills in the air and not in the classroom.

Convair F-102A Delta Dagger

First flight: October 24, 1953

Power: Pratt and Whitney 5307kg/11,700lb (7802kg/17,200lb afterburning) thrust J57P-23 turbojet

Armament: Three AIM-4C Falcon infra-red homing air-to-air missiles and one AIM-26A Nuclear Falcon or three AIM-4A semi-active radar homing and three AIM-4C infra-red air-to-air missiles

Size: Wingspan – 11.62m/38ft 1.5in
Length – 20.84m/68ft 5in
Height – 6.46m/21ft 2.5in
Wing area – 61.45m^2/661.5sq ft

Weights: Empty – 8630kg/19,050lb
Maximum take-off – 14,288kg/31,500lb

Performance: Maximum speed – 1328kph/825mph
Ceiling – 16,460m/54,000ft
Range – 2173km/1350 miles
Climb – 5304m/17,400ft per minute

TOP: **This F-102A served with the 82nd Fighter Interception Squadron on Okinawa, Japan, and bears a typical camouflage scheme of the era.** ABOVE: **With its internal missile bays open, this F-102 shows some of the armament that made the Delta Dagger such a potent interceptor.**

Convair F-106 Delta Dart

Initially designated F-102B, the F-106 was conceived as the ultimate interceptor. Delayed engine and electronic development for what became the F-106 forced the development of the interim F-102. While the F-102 was developed, the USAF refined its requirements for the new super-fighter – it had to intercept enemy aircraft in all weathers up to 21,335m/70,000ft and be capable of Mach 2 interceptions up to 10,670m/35,000ft. Prototype flights between December 1956 and February 1957 were disappointing and the USAF almost scrapped the whole programme. Instead they reduced the order from

1000 aircraft to 350 to save spiralling costs. Engine and avionics improvements brought the F-106 up to an acceptable standard and the type entered operational service as the F-106A in October 1959. Production ceased in December 1960 but the F-106 remained in front-line service for more than 20 years thanks to constant updating programmes – it was finally phased out of Air National Guard service in 1988.

The F-106's Hughes MA-1 fire control system essentially managed all interceptions from radar-lock to missile firing while the pilot simply acted as a

systems supervisor. Among the weaponry were two devastating Genie nuclear-tipped air-to-air missiles carried in an internal bomb-bay, which the computer would instruct the pilot to arm just prior to firing.

From 1973 F-106s were equipped with a multi-barrel "Gatling-gun" rotary cannon, reflecting the realization that fighters might once again need to tackle an enemy in close combat and not just from a stand-off position using long-range missiles. Pilots say the F-106 was a delight to fly and at its peak the F-106 equipped 13 US Air Defense Command squadrons.

TOP: **A fine air-to-air photograph of a New Jersey Air National Guard F-106A. The bump on the fuselage forward of the windscreen is a retractable infra-red detector.** ABOVE: **This F-106 is believed to have been used by NASA for some unmanned drone missions after its retirement from USAF Air Defense Command.**

Convair F-106A Delta Dart

First flight: December 26, 1956

Power: Pratt & Whitney 11,113kg/24,500lb afterburning-thrust P-17 turbojet engine

Armament: One 20mm/0.78in cannon, four Falcon AAMs, plus two Genie unguided nuclear rockets

Size: Wingspan – 11.67m/38ft 2.5in
Length – 21.55m/70ft 8.75in
Height – 6.18m/20ft 3.3in
Wing area – 64.8m²/697.8sq ft

Weights: Empty – 10,800kg/23,814lb
Maximum take-off – 17,350kg/38,250lb

Performance: Maximum speed – 2393kph/1487mph
Ceiling – 17,680m/58,000ft
Range – 3138km/1950 miles with external tanks
Climb – 9144m/30,000ft per minute

Dassault Mystère/Super Mystère

LEFT: **Unusually, the Mystère IVs that joined the Armée de l'Air in 1955 were funded by the USA under a NATO Assistance Programme.**
BELOW: **A Super Mystère B2 of an Armée de l'Air "Tiger squadron" – not a usual paint scheme.**

Developed from the Dassault Ouragan, France's first jet fighter, the Mystère was essentially an Ouragan with swept wing and tail surfaces, and first flew in 1951.

The production version, the Mystère II, was one of the first swept-wing aircraft in production in Western Europe and entered Armée de l'Air service between 1954 and 1956, powered by the SNEC-MA Atar, the first French turbojet engine to be used in military aircraft. A Mystère IIA was the first French aircraft to break Mach 1 in controlled flight (in a dive), on October 28, 1952. The Armée de l'Air ordered 150 Mystère IICs and the last was delivered in 1957, by which time the type was already being relegated to advanced training duties. Even as the Mystère was becoming operational, the better Mystère IV was already flying. Mystère IIs remained in use as advanced trainers until 1963.

The Mystère IV was a new aircraft, having few common parts with the Mk II and had a new oval-section fuselage, thinner wings with greater sweep, and new tail surfaces. The first prototype was flown in September 1952, powered by an Hispano-built Rolls-Royce Tay 250 turbojet engine, as were the first 50 production examples – later examples were powered by the Hispano-Suiza Verdon. The production contract for 225 Mystère IVAs for the Armée de l'Air was paid for by the United States as part of the NATO Military Assistance Program. The first production Mystère IVA flew in late May 1954 and the type entered

service with the Armée de l'Air the following year. The Mystère IVA remained a first-line fighter with the Armée de l'Air until the early 1960s but continued to serve as an operational trainer until 1980.

SIxty Verdon-powered Mystère IVAs ordered by the French were sold on to Israel and the first batch of 24 arrived in April 1956, just in time for the war in October. In the hands of skilled Israeli pilots, they proved more than a match for Egyptian MiG-15s. The Indian Air Force also bought 110 all-new production Verdon-powered Mystère IVAs. First delivered in 1957, they were used in the close-support role during the 1965 Indo-Pakistan War.

The ultimate Mystère was the Super Mystère, which like the Mystère IV was largely a new aircraft. It was bigger and heavier than previous Mystères and was the first European production aircraft capable of transonic flight. The first prototype flew in March 1955 and had wings with a 45-degree sweepback and an F-100-like oval air intake. The prototype exceeded Mach 1 in level flight the day after it first took to the air. A total of 180 Super Mystère B2s were built for the Armée de l'Air, and the last was delivered in 1959. They were relegated to the attack role once the Mirage III was available and remained in French service

until late 1977. In 1958, 36 Super Mystères bought by the French were sold on to the Israelis who used them to counter the MiG-19s favoured by Arab nations. In the early 1970s, the Israelis upgraded surviving Super Mystères by retrofitting a non-afterburning Pratt & Whitney J52-P8A turbojet engine and 12 of these uprated Super Mystères were sold to Honduras, who operated them until 1989, when the operational career of the Mystère series came to an end.

Dassault Mystère IVA

First flight: February 23, 1951 (Mystère prototype)
Power: Hispano-Suiza 3500kg/7716lb-thrust Verdon 350 turbojet engine
Armament: Two 30mm/1.18in cannon, plus two 454kg/1000lb bombs or 12 rockets
Size: Wingspan 11.12m/36ft 6in
  Length – 12.85m/42ft 2in
  Height – 4.6m/15ft 1in
  Wing area – 32m^2/344.46sq ft
Weights: Empty – 5886kg/12,950lb
  Maximum take-off – 9500kg/20,944kg
Performance: Maximum speed – 1120kph/696mph
  Ceiling – 15,000m/49,200ft
  Range – 912km/570 miles
  Climb – 2700m/8860ft per minute

Dassault–Breguet Mirage 2000

In December 1975 Dassault got the green light to proceed with what became the Mirage 2000 programme to develop a replacement for the Mirage F.1. With this design, Dassault revisited the delta wing shape of the Mirage III series and brought greatly improved manoeuvrability and handling thanks to fly-by-wire systems and a much greater knowledge of aerodynamics. Although the Mirage 2000 looks very similar to the Mirage III series, it is an entirely new aircraft. The prototype first flew in March 1978 and service deliveries began in 1983. For its secondary ground-attack role, the Mirage 2000 carries laser guided missiles, rockets and bombs.

The last of 136 single-seat Mirage 2000Cs were delivered to the Armée de l'Air in 1998 but foreign orders for this very capable fighter were secured some years before. Abu Dhabi, Greece, Egypt, Peru and India all operate export 2000 models.

There is a two-seat version of this aircraft, the 2000N, which has nuclear stand-off capability. The Mirage 2000D, derived from the Mirage 2000N operated by the French Air Force, is a two-seater air-to-ground attack aircraft that carries air-to-ground high precision weapons which can be fired at a safe distance, by day or by night. Its navigation and attack systems enable it to fly in any weather conditions, hugging the terrain at a very low altitude.

A modernized multi-role version, the Mirage 2000-5, was also offered from 1997, featuring improved more powerful

ABOVE: **The Mirage 2000 is a fine example of a very good aircraft being developed into a series of specialist variants.** BELOW: **The aircraft's M53-P2 turbofan generates 9917kg/21,835lb of afterburning thrust.**

radar, more powerful engine and compatibility with the Matra Mica air-to-air missile. The Mirage 2000-5 is a single-seater or two-seater fighter and differs from its predecessors mainly in its avionics and its new multiple target air-to-ground and air-to-air firing procedures. The aircraft has Hands On Throttle and Stick control, a Head-Up Display and five cathode ray tube multi-function Advanced Pilot Systems Interface (APSI) displays. The combined head-up/head-level display presents data relating to flight control, navigation, target engagement and weapon firing. The Taiwan Republic of China Air Force operates 60 Mirage 2000-5s while Qatar took delivery of 12 in 1997 having sold its Mirage 1s to Spain to finance the purchase.

Mirage 2000 has nine hardpoints for carrying weapon system payloads, five on the fuselage and two on each wing. The single-seat version is also armed with two internally mounted high-firing rate 30mm/1.18in guns. Air-to-air weapons include the MICA multi-target air-to-air intercept and combat missiles and the Matra Magic 2 missiles. The aircraft can carry four MICA missiles, two Magic missiles and three drop tanks simultaneously. The Mirage 2000-5 can fire the Super 530D missile or the Sky Flash air-to-air missile as an alternative to the MICA.

The Mirage 2000 is equipped with a multi-mode doppler radar which provides multi-targeting capability in the air defence role, and the radar also has a look down/shoot down mode of operation. The radar can simultaneously detect up to 24 targets and carry out track-while-scan on the eight highest priority threats, an invaluable tool for a pilot.

Armée de l'Air Mirage 2000Cs served as part of the UN peacekeeping force over Bosnia and Kosovo.

TOP: **A single-seat Mirage 2000C fighter is seen here armed with Matra Magic and Matra Super 530S air-to-air missiles.** ABOVE: **The Mirage 2000 is an incredibly agile aircraft which always thrills crowds.** BELOW: **The stork emblem on the tail of this two-seat Mirage 2000B identifies it as an aircraft of Escadron de Chasse 1/2 Cigognes.**

Dassault-Breguet Mirage 2000C

First flight: March 10, 1978

Power: SNECMA 9917kg/21,835lb afterburning thrust M53-P2 turbofan

Armament: Two 30mm/1.18in cannon, nine hardpoints capable of carrying 6300kg/13,890lb of weaponry including Super 530D, 530F, 550 Magic, Magic 2 AAMs, bombs and rockets

Size: Wingspan – 9.13m/29ft 11in
Length – 14.36m/47ft 1in   Height – 5.2m/17ft
Wing area – 41m^2/441.4 sq ft

Weights: Empty – 7500kg/16,534lb
Maximum take-off – 17,000kg/37,480lb

Performance: Maximum speed – 2338kph/1452mph
Ceiling – 16,470m/54,000ft
Range – 1850km/1149 miles
Climb – 17,080m/56,000ft per minute

Dassault Etendard and Super Etendard

Dassault's private venture Etendard (standard) was designed to meet the needs of both French national and NATO programmes for new light fighters, reflecting air combat experiences during the Korean War. Dassault clearly adhered to the proven Super Mystère layout, although slightly scaled down, but various versions did not get beyond the prototype stage. Then the Etendard IV drew the attention of the French Navy as a multi-role carrier-based fighter, leading to the development of the Etendard IVM specifically for the Navy – it was the first naval aircraft developed by Dassault.

The Etendard IVM made its maiden flight in May 1958 and between 1961 and 1965, the French Navy took delivery of 69 Etendard IVMs that served on the French carriers *Foch* and

Clemenceau, as well as 21 reconnaissance Etendard IVPs. The Etendard IVMs continued to serve in the French Navy until July 1991, by which time they had logged 180,000 flying hours and made 25,300 carrier landings.

The search for an Etendard replacement led to Dassault proposing the Super Etendard, an updated and much improved aircraft based on the Etendard IVM but a 90 per cent new design. Designed for strike and interception duties, it featured the more powerful Atar 8K-50 engine and a strengthened structure to withstand higher-speed operations. The weapons system was improved through the installation of a modern navigation and combat management system centred on a Thomson multi-mode radar. The wing had a new leading edge and revised flaps which, with the newer engine, eased take-off with greater weight than the Etendard.

The aircraft prototype made its maiden flight on October 28, 1974 and the first of 71 production aircraft were delivered from mid-1978, again for service on the aircraft carriers *Foch* and *Clemenceau*. 100 Super Etendards were planned for the Navy but spiralling costs called for a reduction of the order. Armed with two 30mm/1.18in cannon, the Super Etendard could carry a variety of weaponry on its five hard points, including two Matra Magic air-to-air missiles, four pods of 18 68mm/2.68in

ABOVE: **The Etendard was designed to reflect the experiences of air combat during the Korean War.** BELOW: **The Etendard IVP reconnaissance version was in Aeronavale service for almost three decades.**

LEFT: **The Super Etendard was developed from the Etendard but was a 90 per cent new aircraft.**
BELOW: **This Aeronavale Super Etendard was photographed at Boscombe Down in 1992.**
BOTTOM: **Thanks to a programme of upgrades, French Super Etendards will remain in service until 2008, by which time the Rafale will have replaced the type.**

rockets, a variety of bombs or two Exocet anti-ship missiles. A number were also modified to carry the Aérospatiale ASMP nuclear stand-off bomb.

The Argentine Navy's use of the Super Etendard/Exocet combination during the Falklands War of 1982 proved devastating against British ships – Argentina had ordered 14 Super Etendards from Dassault in 1979 but only five had been delivered from 1981. These five strike fighters, with pilots unwilling to engage the agile British Harriers in air combat, were nevertheless a very potent element of the Argentine inventory.

A handful of Super Etendards were supplied to Iraq in October 1983 as the Iraqis were desperate to cripple Iran by attacking tankers in the Persian Gulf with Exocets. Around 50 ships were attacked in the Gulf in 1984, the majority of the actions apparently carried out by Iraqi Super Etendards.

Production of the Super Etendard ended in 1983 but from 1992 a programme of structural and avionics upgrading was undertaken to extend the service life of the "fleet" until 2008.

ABOVE: **The Etendard IVP had a fixed refuelling probe and cameras in the nose. It could also carry a "buddy pack" and act as an inflight refuelling tanker.**

Dassault Super Etendard

First flight: October 28, 1974
Power: SNECMA 5000kg/11,025lb afterburning thrust Atar 8K-50 turbojet engine
Armament: Two 30mm/1.18in cannon, plus 2100kg/4630lb of weapons, including Matra Magic air-to-air missiles, AM39 Exocet ASMs, bombs and rockets
Size: Wingspan – 9.6m/31ft 6in
Length – 14.31m/46ft 11.5in
Height – 3.86m/12ft 8in
Wing area – 28.4m²/305.71sq ft
Weights: Empty – 6500kg/14,330lb
Maximum take-off – 12,000kg/26,455lb
Performance: Maximum speed – 1205kph/749mph
Ceiling – 13,700m/44,950ft
Range – 650km/404 miles
Climb – 6000m/19,685ft per minute

Dassault Mirage F1

The swept-wing F1 multi-role fighter was developed as a successor to the excellent Mirage III and first flew just before Christmas in 1966. The first customer for the single-seat F1 was the French Armée de l'Air, who received the first of 100 F1Cs in May 1973. Later deliveries to the same service were of the F1C-200 version, which had a fixed probe for inflight refuelling. The F1 could carry a large offensive/defensive payload, handled well at low altitude and had a very impressive climb rate – all essential for truly great fighters. The aircraft's very good short take-off and landing performance (it could take-off and land within 500–800m/1640–2625ft) was produced by the wing's high lift system of leading-edge droops and large flaps.

The Mirage F1's turn-around time between missions was impressive, due to its onboard self-starter and a high-pressure refuelling system which filled all onboard tanks within six minutes. The F1 could be airborne within two minutes, courtesy of a special self-propelled ground vehicle that kept the aircraft's systems "alive", cooled or heated as required, and ready to go. The ingenious vehicle also carried a cockpit sunshade on a telescopic arm so the pilot could sit at readiness in the cockpit for hours in the highest of temperatures. As soon as the aircraft started to taxi, the umbilicals were automatically ejected and the aircraft was on its own.

TOP: **A quarter of a century after it first flew, the Mirage F1 is still a very effective fighter in a number of air force inventories.** ABOVE: **This French Air Force F1 sports a very striking squadron anniversary paint scheme.**

The F1's Thomson-CSF Cyrano IV radar, housed in the glass-reinforced plastic nose, enabled the F1 pilot to intercept targets at all altitudes, even those flying at low level. A fire-control computer could then fire the appropriate weapons automatically, if required.

Although production of the F1 ceased in 1989, the F1 continues to be a key aircraft in French air defence strategy and upgrades of the popular jet will undoubtedly keep it in service with other air forces well beyond 2010.

France has exported the F1 to Ecuador, Greece, Jordan, Morocco, Spain, South Africa, Libya and Iraq. The last country, however, fielded the type without success during the Gulf War. The F1A was also built under licence by Atlas Aircraft in South Africa.

TOP LEFT: **The Spanish Air Force (Ejercito del aire) were a major export customer of the F1. The Spanish fleet was expanded in the 1990s by the acquisition of Qatar's F1 fleet.** TOP RIGHT: **The F1's stalky undercarriage is a distinctive identifying feature of the type.** ABOVE: **Jordan's F1s were gradually replaced by F-16s in the early 2000s.** BELOW: **The F1C-200 is equipped with a fixed but detachable inflight refuelling probe.**

Dassault Mirage F1

First flight: December 23, 1966

Power: One SNECMA 49kN/11,025lb (70.2kg/15,785lb afterburning) Atar 9K-50 turbojet engine

Armament: Two 30mm/1.17in DEFA 553 cannons in fuselage and up to 4000kg/8818lb of other weapons, including AIM-9 Sidewinder or Magic air-to-air missiles on wingtips or R.530 or Super 530F radar-guided air-to-air missiles on underwing or centreline hardpoints

Size: Wingspan – 8.4m/27ft 7in, excluding wingtip missiles
Length – 15.3m/50ft 3in   Height – 4.5m/14ft 9in
Wing area – 25m²/269.1sq ft

Weights: Empty – 7400kg/16,315lb
Maximum loaded – 16,200kg/35,715lb

Performance: Maximum speed – 2338kph/1452mph
Ceiling – 20,008m/65,600ft
Range – 900km/560 miles with full weapon load, unrefuelled
Climb – 12,789m/41,931ft per minute

Dassault Mirage III family

The delta-wing Mirage III is certainly one of the greatest ever combat aircraft and was produced in greater numbers than any other European fighter. The success of this aircraft brought France to the forefront of the military aircraft industry. It started as a Dassault private venture project and first flew in November 1956, having benefited from the testing of the small Mirage I experimental delta aircraft. After some refinements to the wing design, in October 1958 it became the first western European aircraft to reach Mach 2 in level flight. The aircraft's capability soon caught the attention of the French Armée de l'Air, who quickly ordered the high-performance aircraft as a new fighter for their inventory.

Foreign air forces were also very interested in the Mirage III and orders from Israel and South Africa followed in late 1960. By now the first production aircraft, the Mirage IIIC single-seat air defence fighter, was coming off the production line for the Armée de l'Air and the first were delivered in July 1961. Equipped with the Cyrano AI radar, the Mirage IIIC was armed with two 30mm/1.18in cannon and air-to-air missiles. Some of Israel's IIICs, well used in combat, were sold to Argentina in 1982, a country which already operated that type.

The Mirage IIIE was a long-range fighter-bomber version powered by the SNECMA Atar 9C turbojet. While the IIIC was a dedicated interceptor, the IIIE was designed and equipped for both air defence and all-weather ground attack and French versions were equipped to carry a nuclear bomb. It was widely exported and was also built under licence in Australia and Switzerland. Although France has retired its Mirage IIIs, many air forces still operate the type, having upgraded it in many ways – Swiss and Brazilian IIIs, for example, have acquired canard wings to enhance their handling.

It was the IIIE that spawned the Mirage 5 ground-attack fighter, basically a simplified version of the IIIE, designed as

ABOVE: **The Belgian Air Force operated over 70 Mirages – a Mirage 5 is here seen nearing the end of its landing roll with braking parachute deployed.**
BELOW: **This 1966 photograph features an Armée de l'Air Mirage IIIC of Escadre de Chasse 3/2 "Alsace". The fin of this early paint scheme IIIC carries the Alsace coat of arms.**

a daytime clear weather ground-attack fighter in response to an Israeli Air Force request. The need for sophisticated radar was considered to be not so great in the Middle East and when the Israeli Mirage 5 first flew in May 1967 it was minus the Cyrano radar. The delivery to Israel was stopped for political reasons by President de Gaulle and the aircraft instead served as the Mirage 5F in the Armée de l'Air. Israel then decided to go it alone and developed their Mirage III into the Kfir.

Some 450 Mirage 5s were, however, exported to other nations and more advanced avionics were offered later. Belgium built their own Mirage 5s and upgraded them in the 1990s to keep them flying until 2005.

The Mirage 50 multi-mission fighter was created by installing the more powerful Atar 9K-50 engine in a Mirage 5 airframe. It first flew in April 1979 and boasted Head-Up Displays and a more advanced radar than the Mirage III. Chile and Venezuela both ordered Mirage 50s. Dassault offers the Mirage 50M upgrade for existing Mirage IIIs and 5s but several operator nations have undertaken local upgrade programmes with improved avionics and the addition of canard foreplanes.

In the 1967 and 1973 Arab-Israeli wars, the Israeli Mirage IIIs outclassed Arab-flown MiGs and generated lots of export sales, but Mirage pilots admit that the type did not have a great sustained turn capability due to the aerodynamic idiosyncrasies of the delta wing. Indeed three Mirages were shot down by Iraqi Hunters during the Six Day War of 1967. Nevertheless, the Mirage III series gave many air forces their first fighters capable of flying at twice the speed of sound and many upgraded examples around the world will be flying until at least 2005.

TOP: **The Swiss Air Force operated fighter and reconnaissance versions of the Mirage III.**

ABOVE: **The Mirage III was undoubtedly one of the finest fighting aircraft ever built.**

ABOVE: **Two-seat trainer versions were supplied to most Mirage III/5 export customers.**

Dassault Mirage IIIC

First flight: November 18, 1956

Power: SNECMA 6000kg/13,228lb afterburning thrust Atar 9C turbojet engine

Armament: Two 30mm/1.18in cannon, plus two Sidewinder air-to-air missiles and one Matra R.530 air-to-air missile

Size: Wingspan – 8.22m/27ft
Length – 14.75m/48ft 5in
Height – 4.5m/14ft 9in
Wing area – 35m²/375sq ft

Weights: Empty – 6575kg/14,495lb
Maximum take-off – 12,700kg/27,998lb

Performance: Maximum speed – 2112kph/1320mph
Ceiling – 20,000m/65,615ft
Range – 1610km/1000 miles
Climb – 5000m/16,400ft per minute

Dassault Rafale

Even as Mirage 2000 was entering service in the early 1980s, a successor was already being sought to be the prime French Air Force fighter. After France withdrew from what became the Eurofighter programme, attention was then focused on Dassault's Avion de Combat Experimentale (ACX) which first flew on July 4, 1986 and was later designated Rafale A.

This demonstrator aircraft was used to test the basic design including the airframe, powerplant and the fly-by-wire system.

Directly derived from the slightly (3 per cent) larger Rafale A demonstrator, production Rafales appeared in three versions – the single-seat air defence Rafale C, the two-seater trainer/multi-role Rafale B and the single-seat Rafale M fighter for the Navy. The three versions were fitted with the same engines (the SNECMA M88-2), navigation/attack system, aircraft management system and flight control systems. The cockpit had Hands On Throttle

ABOVE: The Rafale is a twin-engined highly advanced fighter. The two-seat Rafale B can be a trainer or multi-role combat aircraft. LEFT: The Rafale's delta wing is complemented by small canards forward of the leading edge, resulting in outstanding agility.

and Stick (HOTAS) controls, a wide-angle Head-up Display (HUD), two multi-function display (MFD) monitors showing all flight and instrument information, and a helmet-mounted weapons sight. Voice recognition is planned to feature in future versions so the pilot will be able to issue orders to the aircraft simply by using his or her voice.

All three versions had the same 213kph/132mph approach speed and take-off/landing run of less than 400m/1312ft made possible by complementing the delta wing with canard foreplanes, which together optimize aerodynamic efficiency and stability control without impeding the pilot's visibility. The materials employed and the shapes that make up the aircraft were both carefully selected to minimize the aircraft's electro-magnetic and infra-red signature to make it as "stealthy" as possible. Carbon and Kevlar composites, superplastic-formed diffusion-bonded titanium and aluminium-lithium alloys have all been used in this aircraft.

The first production aircraft, Rafale B1, flew in December 1998 with a total of up to 234 aircraft to be delivered to the

French Air Force from 1998 to 2005. The total programme for the French Air Force and Navy is set at 294 aircraft.

The single-seat Rafale C (first flight May 19, 1991) is an air defence fighter with fully integrated weapons and navigation systems. Making full use of the latest technology, it is capable of outstanding performance on multiple air-to-air targets.

The two-seat multi-role Rafale B first took to the air on April 30, 1993 and retained most of the elements of the single-seater version, including its weapons and navigation system. The Rafale B could undertake an operational mission with just a pilot as crew or with a pilot and a weapons system operator. In Armée de l'Air service the B model is intended to replace the popular ground-attack Jaguar and can carry up to 8000kg/17,637lb of weaponry – in the air-to-air role this will include up to eight Matra Mica AAM missiles.

The Rafale M was ordered to replace the French Navy's ageing fleet of F-8 Crusaders, and is a single-seat fighter strengthened for seaborne use with a toughened undercarriage, arrester hook and catapult points for deck launches. This navalized Rafale first flew in December 1991. The first flight of a production Rafale M took place in July 1999, and on the same day a Rafale M prototype landed on France's nuclear-powered aircraft carrier *Charles de Gaulle*. The Navy's first Rafale unit of 12 aircraft was scheduled to embark on the carrier in 2002, the first of a total of 60 aircraft planned for the French Navy.

The first Rafale produced for the French Air Force, a two-seater, was handed over in December 1999.

ABOVE: **The Rafale's two engines generate an impressive combined thrust of 17764kg/39,110lb.** LEFT: **Proudly displaying the test flight running total, this navalized Rafale M is displayed with its range of available weaponry.**

RIGHT: **An early Rafale pictured the year after the type's test flight.** BELOW: **The Rafale was designed to be central to the French fighter force. Until the type is ready to equip the French Air Force and Navy, existing types such as the Mirage F1 and Mirage 2000 will continue to serve.**

Dassault Rafale C

First flight: May 19, 1991

Power: Two SNECMA 8882kg/19,555lb afterburning thrust M88-2 augmented turbofans

Armament: One 30mm/1.18in cannon, maximum of 14 hardpoints carrying a weapons load of up to 6000kg/13,228lb including eight Matra Mica AAMs, ASMP stand-off nuclear missile and other munitions

Size: Wingspan – 10.9m/35ft 9in
Length – 15.3m/50ft 2in
Height – 5.34m/17ft 6in
Wing area – 46m²/495.1sq ft

Weights: Empty – 9060kg/19,973lb
Maximum take-off – 21,500kg/47,399lb

Performance: Maximum speed – 2125kph/1320mph
Ceiling – 20,000m/65,620ft
Range – 1850km/1150 miles with maximum weapon load
Climb – not published

LEFT: **Royal Navy Sea Hornet F.20s of No.728 Squadron, Fleet Air Arm.** BELOW: **Designed for combat in the Pacific Theatre, the Hornet arrived before the end of World War II. The photograph shows PX210, the first production Hornet F.1.**

de Havilland Hornet

Following the success of the Mosquito, the de Havilland design team turned their thoughts to a scaled-down single-seat Mosquito capable of taking on Japanese fighters in the Pacific. Very long range was a major feature of the design that came to be known as the Hornet and streamlining was seen as one way of achieving that. Rolls-Royce were involved from the outset and were responsible for developing Merlin engines with a

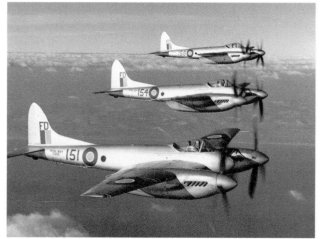

reduced frontal area to lessen the drag on the aircraft. Although inspired by the Mosquito, the Hornet was a completely new aircraft – the main similarity between the two types was the plywood-balsa-plywood technique for building the wooden fuselage. The Hornet wing also differed from that of the Mosquito in that it was made

of wood and metal – the Hornet was the first aircraft in which wood was cemented to metal using the pioneering Redux adhesive.

Geoffrey de Havilland Jr took the Hornet into the air for the first time in July 1944. Although the first production aircraft were delivered to the RAF in April 1945, the type did not see action in World War II. In fact the first RAF Hornet squadron, No.64, was not formed until May 1946. Hornets defended UK air space until replaced by Meteor 8s in 1951, but from 1949 they were switched from interceptor to intruder duties.

Most RAF Hornets joined the Far East Air Force in early 1951 for action in Malaya. Equipped with rocket projectiles or bombs, the Hornets proved very effective against terrorist targets in the jungle. The Hornets of No.45 Squadron became the last piston-engined fighters in RAF service and were finally replaced by Vampires in 1955.

A naval version was considered from the start and the production Sea Hornet had folding wings, arrester hook, plus naval radio and radar, as well as landing gear modified for deck landings. Sea Hornets appeared in day and two-seat

nightfighter versions, the latter version proving to be considerably slower. The Fleet Air Arm's No.801 Squadron operated Sea Hornet F.20s from the carrier HMS *Implacable* between 1949 and 1951.

ABOVE: **The engines dominated the Hornet from any perspective – a Hornet F.3 of the RAF Linton-on-Ouse Station Flight.** LEFT: **The Hornet/ Sea Hornet pioneered the use of Redux adhesive in construction – Royal Navy Sea Hornet F.20s.**

de Havilland Hornet F. Mk 3

First flight: July 28, 1944 (prototype)

Power: Two Rolls-Royce 2030hp Merlin 130/131 in-line piston engines

Armament: Four 20mm/0.78in cannon in nose, plus provision for up to 908kg/2000lb of underwing bombs or rockets

Size: Wingspan – 13.73m/45ft
Length – 11.18m/36ft 8in
Height – 4.32m/14ft2in
Wing area – 33.54m^2/361sq ft

Weights: Empty – 5850kg/12,880lb
Maximum take-off – 9493kg/20,900lb

Performance: Maximum speed – 759kph/472mph
Ceiling – 10,675m/35,000ft
Range – 4827km/3000 miles
Climb – 1220m/4000ft per minute

de Havilland Sea Vixen

The Sea Venom's successor in Royal Navy service was the impressive de Havilland Sea Vixen, which, when it first appeared in the early 1950s, was a match for any land-based fighter of the time. It gave the Royal Navy its first swept-wing two-seat all-weather fighter and was developed from the D.H.110 that was designed to meet Royal Navy and Royal Air Force requirements. Although it followed the Vampire/Venom-type twin-boom configuration, this was a

the mainstay of carrier-borne fighter squadrons for a decade. It was the first British interceptor to dispense with guns and was armed only with air-to-air missiles and rockets.

The Sea Vixen FAW. Mk 1 had a hinged radome, power-folding wings and a steerable nosewheel. The novel nose arrangement had the pilot's cockpit off-set to the port side to provide sufficient working space for a radar operator below and behind on the starboard side.

The FAW. Mk 2 was an improved version, either upgraded from Mk 1 standard or built from new. More fuel was carried in the forward sections of the tail-booms, which were extended forward of the wings, and armament for this model was four Red Top air-to-air missiles in place of the Firestreaks carried by the FAW. Mk 1.

Despite the Sea Vixen's late entry into service, the aircraft gave the Royal Navy a formidable all-weather interception and surface-attack capability until the type was finally retired in 1972.

totally modern aircraft. Development delays following the high-profile and tragic 1952 crash of the prototype at Farnborough kept the Sea Vixen from entering Royal Navy Fleet Air Arm service until 1958. The aircraft became operational the following year and was

TOP LEFT: **This weary FAW. Mk 2 shows the extent of wing folding on the type.** ABOVE LEFT: **The Sea Vixen pilot's cockpit sat offset to the port side to make room for the fellow crew member.**

de Havilland Sea Vixen FAW. Mk 2

First flight: September 26, 1951 (D.H.110)
Power: Two Rolls-Royce 5094kg/11,230lb-thrust Avon 208 turbojet engines
Armament: Four Red Top infra-red homing air-to-air missiles, plus two retractable nose pods with 28 51mm/2in rocket projectiles
Size: Wingspan – 15.54m/51ft
Length – 16.94m/55ft 7in
Height – 3.28m/10ft 9in
Wing area – 60.2m²/648sq ft
Weights: Empty – 9979kg/22,000lb
Maximum take-off – 16,793kg/37,000lb
Performance: Maximum speed 1110kph/690mph
Ceiling – 14,640m/48,000ft
Range – 1287km/800 miles
Climb – 12,200m/40,000ft in 8.5 minutes

de Havilland Vampire

The Vampire was Britain's first single-jet fighter and was probably the first aircraft whose designers thought the advent of the jet engine called for a rethink of aircraft layout. While many early jets were just modified ex-propeller-driven airframes, the de Havilland company produced instead a radical twin-boom design to accommodate the new form of propulsion – the jet engine.

The Vampire first flew in September 1943 with Geoffrey de Havilland at the controls, only 16 months after detailed design work began. It arrived too late to see action in World War II but joined RAF squadrons in 1946, becoming the second jet aircraft in Royal Air Force service. When the prototype jet fighter first took to the air it was powered by an engine with 1226kg/2700lb thrust, a far cry from, for example, the 6097kg/13,490lb-thrust Eurojet turbofans that power today's Eurofighter.

In the early post-war years, the Vampires of RAF Fighter Command played a key part in the first-line air defence of the UK, until they were replaced in this role by the Meteor 8 in 1951. By then the Vampire was in widespread use with the RAF's Middle East and Far East Air Forces until it was replaced by the de Havilland Venom, the second of de Havilland's distinctive twin-boom designs.

In December 1945 the world's first deck landing by jet was made by the prototype Sea Vampire, which was the first jet aircraft to go into service with any navy. This version was a modified Vampire F.B.5, strengthened to cope with the extra strain put on airframes during arrester-hook landings. It served in the Royal Navy as a much-needed trainer for the Fleet Air Arm's first generation of jet pilots.

Vampires continued to fly in air forces around the world until the mid-1970s and even into the early 1980s, in the

ABOVE: **LZ551 was an English Electric-built prototype equipped with an arrester hook for deck trials.**

cases of the Dominican Republic and, most famously, Switzerland.

In the early 1950s more than 430 Vampires were licence-built by SNCASE at Marseilles (and named the Mistral) giving France's aviation industry a much-needed post-war shot in the arm. Meanwhile Macchi built 80 in Italy and Switzerland produced 178.

Vampire NF. Mk 10 nightfighters also provided valuable service for the RAF. A total of 95 machines were built and some were later refurbished for sale to the Indian Air Force in the mid-1950s. Privately owned versions continue to fly.

ABOVE: **Britain's first single-engine jet fighter, the Vampire, joined RAF squadrons in 1946. The twin-boom layout was a response to the revolutionary new form of propulsion, the jet engine.** RIGHT: **Vampire F.B.9s of No.8 Squadron RAF pictured over Kenya. The F.B.9 was a special version produced for use in tropical climates and had, among other innovations, much needed cockpit air-conditioning.**

de Havilland Vampire F.I

First flight: September 20, 1943

Power: de Havilland 1408kg/3100lb-thrust Goblin 1 turbojet

Armament: Four 20mm/0.78in cannon in nose

Size: Wingspan – 12.2m/40ft
Length – 9.37m/30ft 9in Height – 2.69m/8ft 10in
Wing area – 24.35m^2/262sq ft

Weights: Empty – 2894kg/6372lb
Maximum take-off – 4760kg/10,480lb

Performance: Maximum speed – 868kph/540mph
Ceiling – 12,500m/41,000ft
Range – 1175km/730 miles
Climb – 1312m/4300ft per minute

Douglas F4D Skyray

German wartime aerodynamics experiments led the post-war US Navy to consider the use of a delta wing for a carrier-borne fighter. In 1947, the Douglas Corporation proposed the delta-winged XF4D-1 and, following US Navy approval, the prototype first flew in January 1951. The F4D's capabilities were evident when, on October 3, 1953, the second prototype set a new world air speed record of 1211.7kph/752.9mph.

Deliveries to the US Navy began in April 1956 and 17 front-line US Navy/ USMC units, plus three reserve units, were eventually equipped with the Skyray.

The F4D-1 had an incredible climb rate for the time and on May 22 and 23, 1958 the Skyray piloted by Major Edward LeFaivre of the US Marine Corps broke five world records for time-to-altitude. This feat led to one US Navy unit, VFAW-3, based at Naval Air Station North Island in California, being part of North American Air Defense Command tasked with defending the USA against expected fleets of Soviet bombers.

This unusual aircraft was finally retired in the late 1960s, having been redesignated F-6A in 1962.

TOP: **This F4D is preserved at the Museum of Naval Aviation at Pensacola, Florida, in the United States.**
ABOVE: **The Skyray was a record-breaker and set a number of records for speed and time-to-altitude.**
BELOW: **Directly influenced by German wartime delta wing research, the Skyray entered US Navy service over a decade after the end of World War II.**

Douglas F4D Skyray

First flight: January 23, 1951
Power: Pratt & Whitney 6577kg/14,500lb afterburning thrust J57-P-8B turbojet engine
Armament: Four 20mm/0.78in cannon, plus up to 1814kg/4000lb of fuel or ordnance on six underwing hardpoints
Size: Wingspan – 10.21m/33ft 6in
Length – 13.93m/45ft 8.25in
Height – 3.96m/13ft
Wing area – 51.75m²/557sq ft
Weights: Empty – 7268kg/16,024lb
Maximum take-off – 11,340kg/25,000lb
Performance: Maximum speed – 1162kph/722mph
Ceiling – 16,765m/55,000ft
Range – 1931km/1200 miles
Climb – 5580m/18,300ft per minute

Eurofighter Typhoon

In the modern world, few nations can "go it alone" and develop a new high-performance fighter aircraft. So in 1983 Britain, France, Germany, Italy and Spain issued a joint requirement for a highly agile single-seat fighter with a secondary ground attack capability. The French withdrew in 1985 to pursue their own indigenous design but the other nations continued with what became Eurofighter.

Development work was split between UK and Germany (33 per cent each), Italy (21 per cent) and Spain (13 per cent). Germany threatened to withdraw from the programme in 1992 unless spiralling costs were pegged. A lower specification Eurofighter was proposed, accepted by all partners, and the programme continued.

Eurofighter first flew in Germany in March 1994 and is optimized for air-dominance performance with high instantaneous and sustained turn rates. Special emphasis has been placed on low wing loading, high thrust-to-weight ratio, excellent all round vision and ease of handling. The use of stealth technology is incorporated throughout the aircraft's basic design and it only needs a 700m/2300ft runway.

Eurofighter's high performance is matched by excellent all round vision and by sophisticated attack, identification and defence systems which include long-range radar, Infra-Red Search and Track, advanced medium and short-range air-to-air missiles and a comprehensive electronic warfare suite to enhance weapons system effectiveness and survivability. As well as the expected chaff and flare dispensers, towed decoys are carried in wingtip pods.

Eurofighter is aerodynamically unstable to provide extremely high levels of agility, reduced drag and enhanced lift. The unstable design cannot be flown by conventional means and the pilot controls the aircraft via a computerized "fly-by-wire" system. The pilot has an advanced cockpit dominated by a wide-angle Head-Up Display and three colour monitors displaying all instrument information and flight data, as well as a helmet-mounted sight for weapon aiming. Direct voice input allows the pilot to control aspects of the flight just by talking to the aircraft.

The Eurojet EJ200 turbofan combines high thrust with low fuel consumption and strength.

ABOVE: **The Eurofighter Typhoon is an excellent example of multi-national industry co-operation. The result is a very high-performance fighter that will equip a number of key European air arms for decades to come.** LEFT: **The Eurofighter Typhoon's two turbofans generate a combined thrust of 18396kg/40,500lb, comparable to that of the F-14 Tomcat. An unladen Eurofighter is, however, half the weight of an empty F-14.**

British Eurofighters will be assembled by BAE Systems from components manufactured by companies in the partner nations. In the other nations the respective partner companies will have their own assembly lines in Munich, Turin and Madrid.

Eurofighter Typhoon

First flight: March 27, 1994
Power: Two EJ200 9198kg/20,250lb afterburning thrust turbofans
Armament: One 27mm/1.05in cannon plus 13 hardpoints carrying up to 6500kg/14,330lb of ordnance including short- and medium-range AAMs plus a range of stand-off weapons, bombs, rockets
Size: Wingspan – 10.95m/35ft 11in
Length – 15.96m/52ft 4in
Height – 5.28m/17ft 7in
Wing area – 50m²/538.2sq ft
Weights: Empty – 9990kg/22,043lb
Maximum take-off – 21,000kg /46,297lb
Performance: Maximum speed – 2020kph/1255mph
Ceiling – 16,775m/55,000ft
Range – 1390km/863 miles
Climb – 10,670m/35,000ft in 2 minutes, 30 seconds

Fiat/Aeritalia G91

In response to a 1953 NATO specification for a light strike fighter with rough field capability that was still capable of 0.92 Mach, Fiat proposed the F-86 Sabre-inspired G91. Despite the loss of the prototype on its first flight (August 9, 1956), an accident that would cause the

French to refuse to purchase the aircraft, the G91 entered production for the Italian Air Force. While the design was intended for use by all the NATO countries, only Italy and Germany initially acquired the design.

The Italian Air Force and the Luftwaffe took delivery of the G91R single-seat tactical reconnaissance/ground attack fighter version in the early 1960s. Dornier undertook some production in Germany historically making the G91 the first jet combat aircraft built in Germany since World War II. Some G91s were later transferred to the Portuguese Air Force in 1965.

The G91Y twin-engined fighter, first seen as a development of the G91R, was really a totally new design capable of carrying much greater military loads over much longer distances. Powered by two General Electric jet engines, the G91Y first flew in December 1966 and deliveries to the Regia Aeronautica took place between 1971 and 1975.

ABOVE: **A G91R of the Portuguese Air Force's Escuadra 121 "Tigres". Portugal operated around 40 of the type.** LEFT: **Resembling a late mark F-86 Sabre, the G91 was a straightforward design said by pilots to be easy to handle in the air.**

Fiat G91R

First flight: August 9, 1956
Power: Fiat/Bristol 2268kg/5000lb thrust Orpheus 803 turbojet
Armament: Four 12.7mm/0.5in machine-guns, plus four underwing pylons for a variety of tactical nuclear weapons, iron bombs, air-to-air missiles and other ordnance
Size: Wingspan – 8.56m/28ft 1in
Length – 10.3m/33ft 9.25in
Height – 4m/13ft 1.25in
Wing area – 16.42m^2/176.74sq ft
Weights: Empty – 3100kg/6838lb
Maximum take-off – 5500kg/12,125lb
Performance: Maximum speed – 1075kph/668mph
Ceiling – 13,100m/42,978ft
Range – 630km/392 miles
Climb – 1827m/5990ft per minute

ABOVE: **The G91T two-seat trainer was developed to give pilots experience of flight at transonic speeds. The pre-unification Federal German Air Force took delivery of 66 trainer versions, 22 built under licence in Germany and the rest by Fiat in Italy.**

Folland/Hawker Siddeley Gnat

Best known as a jet trainer, the Gnat actually began life as a private-venture single-seat fighter, the Midge, which first took to the air in August 1954. While fighters around the world were getting more complex and heavier, the Gnat was designed by W.E.W. Petter as a lightweight jet fighter, making use of the smaller jet engines then available.

Although the British government ordered six Gnats for development flying, the Gnat failed to be adopted as an RAF fighter. By mid-1957 the Gnat's potential as a two-seat trainer was recognized by the RAF, leading to orders for a total of 105 two-seat Gnat trainers for the RAF.

India had, however, been impressed by the Gnat as a fighter and had licence-built 213 of them by 1973. In the Indo-Pakistan war of 1971 the Indian Gnats proved most effective in close combat; then in 1974 Hindustan Aircraft Ltd signed an agreement to produce the Gnat II or Ajit (unconquerable). Finland also operated Gnat fighters between 1958 and 1972.

TOP: **The Gnat is best known as a mount of the world-famous RAF Red Arrows aerobatic team.**
ABOVE: **Indian licence-built Gnats saw action against Pakistan in the early 1970s.** BELOW: **Where it all began – the private-venture Midge that first flew in 1954.**

Folland Gnat 1

First flight: July 18, 1955
Power: Bristol 2050kg/4520lb-thrust Orpheus 701 turbojet engine
Armament: Two 30mm/1.18in Aden cannon, plus underwing hardpoints for 454kg/1000lb bomb load
Size: Wingspan – 6.75m/22ft 2in
Length – 9.06m/29ft 9in
Height – 2.69m/8ft 10in
Wing area – 16.26m^2/175sq ft
Weights: Empty – 2200kg/4850lb
Maximum take-off – 4030kg/8885lb
Performance: Maximum speed – 1150kph/714mph
Ceiling – 15,250m/50,000ft plus
Range – 1900km/1180 miles
Climb – 6096m/20,000ft per minute

Gloster Javelin

The Javelin was the first British combat aircraft designed for the all-weather day and night role and was the first twin-engined delta-wing jet in service anywhere.

The design team began work on the Javelin in 1948 and the type first flew on November 26, 1951. After competitive trials with the de Havilland 110 (which led to the Sea Vixen) in July 1952 Britain's Air Ministry chose the Javelin to equip the RAF's all-weather fighter units. Following the loss of three prototypes in accidents and after much redesign, production finally got under way in 1954.

The Javelin was designed to have the very high performance and long endurance that would enable it to intercept high-speed, high-altitude Soviet bombers. With state-of-the-art electronics and radar, the two-seat Javelin was able to operate day or night in all weather conditions. The Javelin's large delta wing provided good high-altitude performance, while the massive swept vertical tail fin carried a delta tailplane on top which helped keep the aircraft's landing angle-of-attack within safe limits for night and all-weather landings.

When the Mk 1 Javelins entered RAF service in 1956, they were the first of 427 of a type that ultimately appeared in nine versions.

The Mk 2 entered service in August 1957 and had uprated engines (3770kg/8300lb, compared to the 3702kg/8150lb-thrust of the Mk 1) and an improved Westinghouse radar. Next came the T.3 dual control trainer, which had no radar but was armed with 30mm/1.18in guns.

Fifty examples of the pilot-friendly Mk 4 were built and with its all-moving tailplane it was much easier to fly. An extra 1137 litres/250 US gallons of internal tankage in a modified wing was the principal performance improvement on the Mk 5 while the Mk 6 was simply a Mk 5 equipped with American radar.

The Javelin FAW.7 was a major redesign and was produced in greater numbers (142) than the other versions. It boasted the much more powerful 4996kg/11,000lb-thrust Sapphire 203 engines and much-needed missile armament of four Firestreak infra-red homing air-to-air missiles in place of two of the 30mm/1.18in guns. This model entered front-line service in July 1958.

Gloster Javelin F(AW). Mk 1

First flight: November 26, 1951
Power: Two Armstrong Siddeley 3629kg/8000lb-thrust Sapphire ASSa.6 turbojet engines
Armament: Two 30mm/1.18in cannon in each wing
Size: Wingspan – 15.85m/52ft
Length – 17.15m/56ft 3in
Height – 4.88m/16ft
Wing area – 86.12m^2/927sq ft
Weights: Empty – 10,886kg/24,000lb
Maximum take-off – 14,324kg/31,580lb
Performance: Maximum speed – 1141kph/709mph
Ceiling – 16,000m/52,500ft
Range – 1530km/950 miles with drop tanks
Climb – 15,250m/50,000ft (Mk 9) in 9.25 minutes

The Mk 8 had afterburners that increased thrust to 6082kg/13,390lb and the final variant was the Mk 9. This ultimate Javelin was a conversion of existing Mk 7s to Mk 8 standard and an inflight refuelling (IFR) probe. Four No.23 Squadron Javelins demonstrated the usefulness of IFR by flying non-stop to Singapore in 1960. FAW.9s were first delivered to No.25 Squadron at Waterbeach in December 1959.

Javelins were the last aircraft built by the famous Gloster company, and their last product was withdrawn from service in June 1967. At its peak, the Javelin equipped 14 Royal Air Force squadrons.

BELOW: **The Javelin was the world's first twin-engined delta jet fighter in service.**

Grumman F7F Tigercat

In 1941 Grumman began design work on a hard-hitting high-performance twin-engine fighter to operate from the Midway class of US aircraft carriers – the Tigercat. As the Tigercat developed it was apparent that it was going to be heavier and faster than all previous US carrier aircraft. It was also unusual in that it had a tricycle undercarriage,

although it retained the usual arrester hook and folding wings for carrier operations. Even before the prototype flew in December 1943, the US Marine Corps had placed an order for 500 of the F7F-1 version. They wanted to use the Tigercat primarily as a land-based fighter in close support of Marines on the ground. Although deliveries began in April 1944, the big fighter arrived too late to be cleared for use in World War II.

Wartime production had diversified to deliver the F7F-2N nightfighter, which differed from the F7F-1 by the removal of a fuel tank to make way for a radar operator cockpit and the removal of nose armament for the fitting of the radar.

An improved fighter-bomber version was also developed, the F7F-3, and had different engines for more power at altitude, a slightly larger fin and bigger fuel tanks.

Tigercat production continued after the war's end with F7F-3N and F7F-4N nightfighters, both having lengthened noses to house the latest radar and a few of these aircraft were strengthened and equipped for carrier operations. Some F7F-3s were modified for electronic and photographic reconnaissance missions.

Although it missed action in World War II, the Tigercat did see combat with the Marine Corps over Korea. USMC fighter unit VMF(N)-513 was based in Japan when the Korean War broke out. Equipped with Tigercat nightfighters, they went into action immediately as night-intruders and performed valuable service.

The US Marines were the only operators of the Tigercat.

TOP: **The fast and heavy F7F was only used by the US Marines.** ABOVE: **Despite its vintage, the high-performance Tigercat is a popular "warbird", and a number are preserved by collectors in the USA and Europe.** LEFT: **Too late for World War II, the F7F was widely used in the Korean War.**

Grumman F7F-3N

First flight: December 1943 (F7F-1)
Power: Two Pratt & Whitney 2100hp R-2800-34W Double Wasp radial piston engines
Armament: Four 20mm/0.78in cannon in wing roots
Size: Wingspan – 15.7m/51ft 6in
Length – 13.8m/45ft 4in
Height – 5.06m/16ft 7in
Wing area – 42.27m²/455sq ft
Weights: Empty – 7379kg/16,270lb
Maximum take-off – 11,666kg/25,720lb
Performance: Maximum speed – 700kph/435mph
Ceiling – 12,414m/40,700ft
Range – 1609km/1000 miles
Climb – 1380m/4530ft per minute

Grumman F9F Cougar

Grumman, aware of wartime German swept-wing research, had considered a swept-wing version of the F9F in December 1945. In March 1950 the company sought official approval for a swept-wing version of the Panther – Grumman was given the green light for this logical and speedy development of an already successful programme.

Having been granted a contract in March 1951, Grumman tested the first swept-wing aircraft of the F9F family on September 20, 1951. It was different enough from the Panther to warrant the new name F9F-6 Cougar – in fact only the forward fuselage was retained from the original straight-winged aircraft. The wings had 35 degrees sweep and the wingtip fuel tanks were deleted – power was provided by the J48-8 engine with water/alcohol injection giving a thrust of 3289kg/7250lb. The Cougar entered US Navy service in late 1952.

The F9F-7 version, powered by the 2880kg/6350lb J33 engine, reached a production total of 168. The final Cougar version, the F9F-8 with its bigger wing, first flew in December 1953 and in

January 1954 exceeded the speed of sound in a shallow dive – 662 were built. This version was equipped to carry early Sidewinder missiles.

Many Cougars and Panthers were converted for use as target drones, and two-seat trainer versions of the Cougar were still flying in US Navy service in the mid-1970s.

ABOVE: **Two-seat conversion of Cougars flew on with the US Navy in the mid-1970s.**

BELOW: **Benefiting from wartime German swept-wing research, the Cougar was a swept-wing version of the Panther.**

Grumman F9F-8 Cougar

First flight: September 20, 1951 (F9F-6)

Power: Pratt & Whitney 3266kg/7200lb thrust J48-P-8A turbojet

Armament: Two 20mm/0.78in cannon plus 908kg/2000lb of underwing weapons

Size: Wingspan – 10.52m/34ft 6in
Length – 13.54m/44ft 5in, including probe
Height – 3.73m/12ft 3in
Wing area – 31.31m²/337sq ft

Weights: Empty – 5382kg/11,866lb
Maximum take-off – 11,232kg/24,763lb

Performance: Maximum speed – 1041kph/647mph
Ceiling – 15,240m/50,000ft
Range – 1610km/1000 miles
Climb – 1860m/6100ft

Grumman F9F Panther

LEFT: **The folded wings of this F9F-2 betray its origins as a naval fighter.** BELOW: **In the Korean War the Panther flew 78,000 missions.** BOTTOM: **The Panther could carry up to 908kg/2000lb of bombs and rockets beneath its wings.**

The Panther was the US Navy's most widely used jet fighter of the Korean War.

Although it was mainly used in the ground-attack role, it did notch up some air combat successes against North Korean MiGs. On July 3, 1950 a Panther of US Navy unit VF-51 aboard USS *Valley Forge* scored the Navy's first aerial kill of the Korean War when it downed a Yak-9. By the end of the war the F9F had flown 78,000 combat missions.

Grumman's first jet fighter for the US Navy had its origins in the last days of World War II, when the US Navy Fighter Branch drew up a requirement for an all-weather/night radar-equipped carrier-borne fighter. As originally planned, Grumman's proposed XF9F-1 was powered by no less than four jet engines positioned in the wings. The high number of engines was dictated by the low power output of early turbojets. As many engines as this called for a wingspan of almost 17m/55.7ft, which worried Grumman – they knew that their twin-engine Tigercat had already proved somewhat large for carrier operations.

As better powerplants were available, the design was refined and when the prototype flew on November 24, 1947 it was powered by a lone Rolls-Royce Nene engine. The Panther's distinctive 454 litre/120 US gallon wingtip fuel tanks were first tested in February 1948 and were adopted as standard to extend the aircraft's range.

This straight-wing model, now called F9F-2, went into production and was equipping US naval units by May 1949, having completed carrier trials two months earlier.

The most produced Panther was the F9F-5, which featured water injection and the J48 engine of 3175kg/7000lb thrust. A total of 616 of this version were built and delivered between November 1950 and January 1953. Panthers continued in US Navy service until 1958, and in 1966 one batch was reconditioned as fighters for the Argentine Navy. Total Panther production was 1382.

Grumman F9F-2B Panther

First flight: November 24, 1947

Power: Pratt & Whitney 2586kg/5700lb-thrust J42-P-8 turbojet engine (licence-built Rolls-Royce Nene)

Armament: Four 20mm/0.78in cannon, plus underwing weapon load of up to 908kg/2000lb

Size: Wingspan – 11.58m/37ft 11.75in
Length – 11.35m/37ft 3in
Height – 3.45m/11ft 4in
Wing area – 23.22m^2/250sq ft

Weights: Empty – 4533kg/9993lb
Maximum take-off – 8842kg/19,494lb

Performance: Maximum speed – 877kph/545mph
Ceiling – 13,600m/44,600ft
Range – 2177km/1353 miles
Climb – 1567m/5140ft per minute

Grumman F11F Tiger

TOP: **Pleasant to fly and well armed, the F11F was popular with pilots.**
ABOVE: **Like the Folland Gnat, the F11F was a diminutive fighter and the type was easy to operate from carriers.** BELOW: **Continued engine problems plagued the Tiger's short US Navy career.**

While the Grumman Cougar was making its first flight, Grumman designers were already hard at work on a successor derived from the Cougar/Panther family. In the end, a totally new design was undertaken, with high performance in combat a major requirement. The resulting aircraft was the smallest and lightest airplane that could be designed for the dayfighter mission. The reduced size had another advantage – only the wingtips needed to be folded for carrier handling and storage, thus eliminating the need for complex heavy wing-folding gear.

The prototype flew in July 1954 but the overall performance was not enough of an improvement over that of the Cougar – supersonic speed was the goal. The engine manufacturers Wright proposed that an afterburner version of the J-65 (which was a licence-built British Sapphire engine) could be developed and a complete redesign of the aft fuselage and tail surfaces followed. During the long and troubled development period that followed, the aircraft got a new designation – the F11F.

The afterburner problems continued and a de-rated engine was fitted to bring the aircraft into service. As a result, the expected performance was never achieved and production was limited to only 201 aircraft.

The Tiger entered US Navy service in March 1957. Easy to maintain and having pleasant flying qualities, it continued to be plagued by many engine problems. The last US Navy Tigers were phased out by April 1961, after only four years of service and were replaced by F-8 Crusaders.

Grumman F11F-1

First flight: July 30, 1954
Power: Wright 3379kg/7450lb-thrust J65-W-18 turbojet engine
Armament: Four 20mm/0.78in cannon and four Sidewinder air-to-air missiles under wings
Size: Wingspan – 9.64m/31ft 7.5in
Length – 14.31m/46ft 11.25in
Height – 4.03m/13ft 2.75in
Wing area – 23.23m²/250sq ft
Weights: Empty – 6091kg/13,428lb
Maximum take-off – 10,052kg/22,160lb
Performance: Maximum speed – 1207kph/750mph
Ceiling – 12,770m/41,900ft
Range – 2044km/1270 miles
Climb – 1565m/5130ft per minute

Grumman F-14 Tomcat

Despite its age, the swing-wing, twin-engine Grumman F-14 Tomcat is still one of the world's most potent interceptors. Its primary missions, in all weathers, are air superiority, fleet air defence and, more recently, precision strikes against ground targets. Continued developments and improvements have maintained its capabilities to the extent that it is still a potent threat and an effective deterrent to any hostile aircraft foolish enough to threaten US Navy aircraft carrier groups. Its mix of air-to-air weapons is unmatched by any other interceptor type, and its radar is the most capable long-range airborne interception radar carried by any fighter today. With its mix of weapons, it can attack any target at any altitude from ranges between only a few hundred feet to over 160km/100 miles away. It is already a classic fighter.

The F-14 had its beginnings in the early 1960s when Grumman collaborated with General Dynamics on the abortive F-111B, the carrier-based escort fighter version of the F-111. Even before the F-111B cancellation took place, Grumman began work on a company-funded project known as Design 303, a carrier-borne aircraft for the air superiority, escort fighter and deck-launched interception role.

Having flown for the first time on December 21, 1970, the first two US Navy F-14 squadrons were formed in 1972 and

ABOVE: **Wings sweeping back for high-speed flight – the F-14 is over three decades old but is still one of the finest interceptors in service today.**

went to sea in 1974, making the Tomcat the first variable geometry carrier-borne aircraft in service. Its variable-geometry wings are designed for both speed and greater stability. In full forward-sweep position, the wings provide the lift needed for slow-speed flight, especially needed during carrier landings. In swept-back position, the wings blend into the aircraft, giving the F-14 a dart-like configuration for high-speed, supersonic flight. Only a handful of swing-wing types are in service.

The F-14 Tomcat was designed to carry a million dollar missile, the AIM-54 Phoenix, and is the only aircraft that is armed with the AIM-54. With a range of over 200km/120 miles the AIM-54 gives the Tomcat a very long-range punch. Enemy aircraft can be engaged before the Tomcat even appears on their radar screens. Less expensive Sidewinders are also carried for close air fighting.

The F-14B, introduced in November 1987, incorporated new General Electric F-110 engines. A 1995 upgrade program was initiated to incorporate new digital avionics and weapons system improvements to strengthen the F-14s multi-mission capability. The vastly improved F-14D, delivered from 1990, was a major upgrade with F-110 engines, new APG-71 radar system, Airborne Self Protection Jammer (ASPJ), Joint Tactical Information Distribution System (JTIDS) and Infra-Red Search and Track (IRST). Additionally, all F-14 variants were given precision strike capability using the LANTIRN (Low Altitude Navigation and Targeting Infra-Red for Night) targeting system, night vision compatibility, new defensive countermeasures systems and a new digital flight control system. LANTIRN pods, placed on an external point beneath the right wing, allow the F-14 to drop laser-guided bombs under the cover of darkness. The improved F-14B and F-14D have been built and deployed by the US Navy in modest numbers.

The Tomcat first got to prove itself in combat on August 19, 1981 when two F-14s from the USS *Nimitz* were "intercepted" by two Libyan Sukhoi Su-22 fighter-bombers. The Libyan jets apparently attacked the F-14s and were destroyed with ease. Again on January 4, 1989, two Libyan MiG-23 "Floggers" were engaged by two F-14s and shot down.

Tomcats also saw combat during Operation Desert Storm in 1991, providing top cover protection for bombers and other aircraft, and performing TARPS (Tactical Air Reconnaissance Pod System) missions – the F-14, equipped with TARPS, is the US Navy's only manned tactical reconnaissance platform.

In late 1995, the F-14 Tomcat was used in the bomber role against targets in Bosnia. Nicknamed "Bombcats", the F-14s dropped "smart" bombs while other aircraft illuminated the targets with lasers.

A total of 79 of the type were even exported to Iran before the downfall of the Shah in 1979 and a number were still in service in 2000, having been without the benefit of US technical back-up since 1980.

TOP: **The F-14 earned a much broader audience when it starred in the Hollywood film *Top Gun*.** MIDDLE: **A Tomcat of USS *George Washington*. Note the port of the single 20mm/0.788in cannon low down on the nose just ahead of the cockpit.** ABOVE: **This F-14 of US Navy fighter squadron VF-142 was based on the US Navy carrier USS *Dwight D. Eisenhower*.**

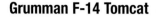

ABOVE: **On the deck of the USS *Nimitz*, this F-14 is about to be moved and prepared for take-off. The F-14 will continue to protect US Navy carrier groups and project American Air Power for the foreseeable future.**

Grumman F-14 Tomcat

First flight: December 21, 1970

Power: Two Pratt & Whitney 9480kg/20,900lb afterburning thrust TF30-P-412A turbofans

Armament: One 20mm/0.78in cannon plus six AIM-7F Sparrow and four AIM-9 Sidewinder AAMs, or six AIM-54A Phoenix long-range AAMs and two AIM-9s, or a variety of air-to-surface weapons up to 6575kg/14,500lb

Size: Wingspan – 19.55m/64ft 1.5in, unswept
Length – 19.1m/62ft 8in
Height – 4.88m/16ft
Wing area – 52.49m^2/565sq ft

Weights: Empty – 18,036kg/39,762lb
Maximum take-off – 31,945kg/70,426lb

Performance: Maximum speed – 2486kph/1545mph
Ceiling – 18,290m/60,000ft
Range – 725km/450 miles
Climb – 18,290m/60,000ft in 2 minutes, 6 seconds

Hawker Hunter

The Hunter, the longest-serving British jet fighter aircraft, was designed to replace the Gloster Meteor in RAF service. Ultimately over 1000 Hunters were built for the RAF in five versions. The prototype flew in July 1951 powered by a 2948kg/6500lb thrust Avon 100 series turbojet and was supersonic in a shallow dive. The Hunter prototype WB188 appeared at the 1951 Farnborough SBAC show, and in April 1952 test pilot Neville Duke took the Hunter through the much-publicized "sound barrier" for the first time. The first production F. Mk 1 flew on May 16, 1953, but this and a further 22 early production aircraft were used for development purposes. The Hunter F.1 entered RAF

service with 43 Squadron in July 1954, replacing their Meteor F.8s, providing the RAF with its long-awaited first transonic fighter. The interceptor capabilities of the Mk 1 were however drastically limited as cannon firing in this mark was restricted to altitudes below 9150m/30,000ft because exhaust gas from the guns caused the engine to flame out. Also, spent cartridge links being ejected by the guns and tumbling along the lower fuselage caused damage or could have even been ingested into the air intakes, so bulbous link collectors were fitted from the F.4 onwards, and were retro-fitted to earlier marks too.

While the F. Mk 1 and the F. Mk 4 that succeeded it were Avon powered, a parallel series of Hunters with the Armstrong Siddeley Sapphire turbojet was developed – the F. Mk 2 and F. Mk 5. The F.2 equipped the RAF's No.257 Squadron from September 1954 and was only produced in limited numbers, despite it not having the flame-out problem of the Mk 1. Both variants were however short-range interceptors and Hawkers

looked at ways to give the Hunter longer legs. The F.4 entered service with 111 Squadron in June 1955, replacing their F.1s. The new model, powered by Avon 115s instead of the problematic Avon 113s of the Mk 1, carried more fuel in strengthened wings which allowed carriage of bombs, rockets and drop tanks.

The Sapphire-powered F.5, otherwise similar to the Mk 4, entered service with 263 Squadron in April 1955 and was the first variant to see active service, being deployed against ground targets in Egypt during the Suez campaign.

Next came the Hunter F. Mk 6 with the 4536kg/10,000lb thrust Avon 203 engine that bestowed a much improved performance and an impressive climb. Although it was only transonic in a dive, the F.6 was built in greater numbers than any other version. Early examples of this high-powered Hunter had a tendency to pitch-up at high speeds, and this was cured by extending the leading edges of the outer portion of the wing, giving the saw-toothed look. F.6s could also scramble more quickly as they used an AVPIN starter system, enabling quicker engine start-up than the cartridge-started early variants. The Hunter F. Mk 6 entered front-line service in October 1956. With better performance at altitude, the Hunter was now able to hold its own with most contemporary fighters but this was shortlived. Britain's V-bombers could climb

beyond its reach and the new American fighters could outperform it. The arrival of the very high-performance Lightning in RAF service spelt the end for the Hunter as an interceptor and the last Fighter Command F.6s were replaced in April 1963. From then on the Hunter's role in the RAF was primarily ground attack, and so the next variant was the FGA.9 which served until 1970 when it was replaced by a mixture of Buccaneers, Phantoms and Harriers. Hunters continued to be used as weapons trainers in the RAF into the 1980s.

The Hunter was of course a major export success and was used by at least 19 foreign air forces. In addition, licence production was carried out in Holland and Belgium. Sweden, Singapore, Denmark and Switzerland all operated Hunters; the latter nation proved to be a long-lived Hunter operator, flying theirs from 1958 until 1995. India made extensive use of the Hunter from 1957 to the early 1980s, and was the first export customer of the type. Participating in the 1965 and 1971 conflicts with Pakistan, the Indian Hunters proved to be a formidable ground attack aircraft and took part in air-to-air combat with Pakistani Sabres and even an F-104. In the 1971 IndoPak war, eight Sabres were claimed by Indian Hunters in air-to-air combat.

ABOVE: **At its peak use, over 1000 Hunters were in service with the RAF.** LEFT: **The Royal Navy used the two-seat Hunters for training pilots of transonic fighter types such as the Scimitar and Sea Vixen.**

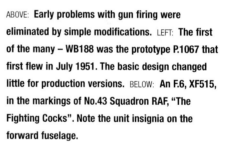

In the Middle East, Hunters were operated by Abu Dhabi, Qatar, Saudi Arabia and Kuwait. Jordan operated Hunters from 1958 until 1974, and their aircraft were the first Arab aircraft to attack Israeli territory in the Six Day War. The Lebanon and Zimbabwe were still operating front-line Hunters in early 2000.

ABOVE: **Early problems with gun firing were eliminated by simple modifications.** LEFT: **The first of the many – WB188 was the prototype P.1067 that first flew in July 1951. The basic design changed little for production versions.** BELOW: **An F.6, XF515, in the markings of No.43 Squadron RAF, "The Fighting Cocks". Note the unit insignia on the forward fuselage.**

Hawker Hunter F. Mk 6

First flight: July 20, 1951 (prototype)
Power: Rolls-Royce 4542kg/10,000lb thrust Avon 203
Armament: Four fixed 30mm/1.18in cannon in removable pack. Provision under wings for two 454kg/1000lb bombs, 5cm/2in or 7.62cm/3in multiple rocket batteries
Size: Wingspan – 10.2m/33ft 8in
Length – 14m/45ft 11in Height – 4.01m/13ft 2in
Wing area – 31.6m²/340sq ft
Weights: Empty – 5795kg/12,760lb
Maximum take-off – 8062kg/17,750lb
Performance: Maximum speed – 1150kph/715mph
Ceiling – 15,707m/51,500ft
Range – 2960km/1840 miles
Climb – 13,725m/45,000ft in 7.5 minutes

Hawker Sea Fury/Fury

The Fury was designed as a lighter, smaller version of the Hawker Tempest to a joint British Air Ministry and Admiralty wartime specification. The land-based Fury first flew in September 1944 but at the war's end RAF interest in the ultimate Hawker piston-engined fighter ceased. Development of the Sea Fury did, however, continue, following the version's test flight in February 1945. This aircraft was essentially a navalized land plane, complete with non-folding wings. The second prototype Sea Fury was a fully navalized aircraft, with folding wings and arrester hook and was powered by a Bristol Centaurus XV.

The production version, the Sea Fury Mk X, began to replace Fleet Air Arm Supermarine Seafires from August 1947. Meanwhile trials with external stores and rocket-assisted take-off equipment led to the Sea Fury FB. Mk 11. It was this aircraft that represented the ultimate development of British piston-engined fighters and the FB.11 proved to be an extremely capable combat aircraft. FAA Sea Furies were among the few British aircraft types that saw combat during the Korean War (1950–3), where they were mainly used in the ground-attack role, operating from HMS *Theseus*, HMS *Ocean*, HMS *Glory* and HMAS *Sydney*. Korea was the first true jet versus jet war but the Sea Fury is known to have destroyed more Communist aircraft than any other non-US type and even shot down a number of North Korean MiGs.

ABOVE: **SR661 was a prototype of the Mk X production version intended to replace Seafires in Fleet Air Arm service.** BELOW: **Certainly the ultimate British piston fighter and considered by some to be the best single-engine piston-powered fighter ever, the Hawker Sea Fury was a very capable fighting aircraft. The example pictured is an FB.11.**

While flying the piston-engined Sea Fury off HMS *Ocean*, Royal Navy Lt Peter Carmichael destroyed a MiG-15 jet and earned himself a place in the history books. "At dawn on August 9, 1952 I was leading a section of four aircraft on a patrol near Chinnampo. We were flying at 1068m/3500ft, looking for rail targets when my Number Two called out, 'MiGs five o'clock – coming in!' Eight came at us from the sun. One came at me head on and I saw his tracer coming over. I managed to fire a burst and then he flashed past. I looked over my shoulder and saw an aircraft going down. When all

LEFT: **The Iraqi Air Force operated a number of land-based Furies in the late 1940s and early 1950s while Pakistan had a number of the type in use into the 1970s.**

my section called in, I knew I'd bagged a MiG! I believe the Sea Fury is the finest single-seat piston fighter ever built."

The Sea Fury, the last piston-engined fighter in RN front-line service, continued flying with Royal Navy Volunteer Reserve units until 1957 and was replaced in FAA service by the Sea Hawk.

Although the RAF rejected the Fury design, a little-known contract with Iraq saw 55 land-based Furies and five two-seat trainers delivered to the Iraqi Air Force between 1948 and 1955. The IAF are known to have used the aircraft in a counter-insurgency role. Pakistan also received Furies and used them in action against India until 1973.

Sea Furies were also exported to Egypt, Burma, Canada, Australia and the Netherlands, where a number were also licence-built by Fokker. At the time of the Cuban Missile Crisis in 1962, Cuba's fighter defence centred on 15 FB.11s, which had been imported in the Batista period.

After their military service a number of these high-performance piston aircraft were snapped up for air racing in the United States, where they set world record speeds.

ABOVE: **The Royal Netherlands Navy was the only other European operator of the Sea Fury. Twenty-two aircraft were exported from the UK while a further 210 were built in Holland by Fokker.** BELOW: **The Royal Australian Navy's HMAS Sydney took its Sea Furies into combat during the Korean War.**

Hawker Sea Fury FB.11

First flight: September 1, 1944
Power: Bristol 2480hp Centaurus 18 two-row sleeve-valve radial engine
Armament: Four 20mm/0.78in cannon in outer wings, plus underwing provision for up to 907kg/2000lb of bombs or rockets
Size: Wingspan – 11.69m/38ft 4.75in, spread 4.9m/16ft 1in, folded
    Length – 10.56m/34ft 8in
    Height – 4.81m/15ft 10in
    Wing area – 26.01m²/280sq ft
Weights: Empty – 4090kg/8977lb
    Maximum take-off – 5669kg/12,500lb
Performance: Maximum speed – 740kph/460mph
    Ceiling – 11,000m/36,000ft
    Range – 1223km /760 miles
    Climb – 1320m/4320ft per minute

LEFT: **The Marut shows what the Third Reich may have been capable of producing.**

Hindustan HF-24 Marut

First flight: June 17, 1961
Power: Two HAL/Rolls-Royce 2200kg/4850lb-thrust Orpheus Mk 703 turbojet engines
Armament: Four 30mm/1.18in cannon, plus retractable pack of 50 68mm/2.68in rockets in belly, plus hardpoints to carry a variety of weapons
Size: Wingspan – 9m/29ft 6.25in
Length – 15.87m/52ft 0.75in
Height – 3.6m/11ft 9.75in
Wing area – 28m^2/301.4sq ft
Weights: Empty – 6195kg/13,658lb
Maximum take-off – 10,908kg/24,048lb
Performance: Maximum speed – 1112kph/691mph
Ceiling – 12,200m/40,000ft
Range – 1000km/620 miles
Climb – 12,200m/40,000ft in 9 minutes 20 seconds

Hindustan HF-24 Marut

The Marut (spirit of the tempest) was the first fruit of the Indian Air Staff's desire for their country to be self-reliant in combat aircraft production. In mid-1950s India, however, there was little expertise in jet aircraft design so the famous Focke-Wulf designer Kurt Tank was invited to create a team (that ultimately included 18 German engineers) to work on the project in India. Design work began in 1957 with the aim of building a Mach-2 capable all-weather multi-role aircraft.

The prototype first flew in June 1961, powered by two Rolls-Royce Bristol Orpheus 703 turbojets and the production aircraft had Indian licence-built Orpheus engines. The Marut finally entered service in April 1967 and was the first supersonic fighter built by a non-superpower.

By late 1975 about 100 aircraft had been delivered and had seen action in the 1971 war against Pakistan, on some occasions dogfighting with enemy F-86 Sabres.

The Marut did not meet expectations as a fighter, but it served the Indian Air Force well until mid-1990.

LEFT: **The Kfir, the ultimate Mirage development.**

IAI Kfir-C7

First flight: October 19, 1970 (Kfir prototype)
Power: IAI/General Electric 8112kg/17,860lb after-burning thrust licence-built J79-JIE turbojet engine
Armament: Two 30mm/1.18in cannon, five underfuselage and two underwing hardpoints for AIM-9 Sidewinder, Python or Shafir air-to-air missiles or anti-radar missiles and bombs
Size: Wingspan – 8.22m/27ft
Length – 15.65m/51ft 4in
Height – 4.55m/14ft 11in
Wing area – 34.8m^2/374.6sq ft
Weights: Empty –7285kg/16,060lb
Maximum take-off – 16,500kg/36,375lb
Performance: Maximum speed – Mach 2.3/2440kph/1515mph
Ceiling – 17,690m/58,000ft
Range – 882km/548 miles
Climb – 13,989m/45,866ft per minute

Israel Aircraft Industries Kfir

The original Kfir (lion cub) prototype that first flew on October 19, 1970 combined a French-built Mirage III airframe with the licence-built GE-J79 afterburning turbojet of the F-4 Phantom II. By the time the Kfir reached production in 1974–5, the airframe was a version of the Israeli-built Mirage 5 (Nesher), equipped with Israeli-built electronics. Only 27 Kfir-C1s were built and 25 were later sold on to the US Navy and Marine Corps for use as "aggressor" aircraft, designated F-21A.

The first of 185 Kfir-C2s entered service in 1976, having first flown in 1974. It sported a canard mounted on the air-intakes. Virtually all C1s were upgraded to C2 standard.

The Kfir-C7 was introduced in 1983 and is an improved upgraded version of the C2, with a more powerful engine and improved performance. It can also carry "smart" weapons, has a sophisticated cockpit and is equipped for inflight refuelling.

The Kfir, widely considered to be the most potent development of the Mirage, is expected to be phased out of IAF service in the early 2000s.

Lavochkin La-11

This aircraft was among the last Soviet piston-engined fighters produced and emerged into a world of jet aircraft. Developed from the earlier Lavochkin La-9, the La-11 was designed to escort Soviet bombers on their long missions. Although it had the same engine and the wing was similar to that of the La-9, other changes were incorporated. Auxiliary fuel tanks were added to the wingtips and the earlier aircraft's distinctive underbelly oil cooler was built into the engine cowling. Armament was reduced from four to three 23mm/0.9in cannon.

The new aircraft first flew in late 1944 and remained in production until 1951 by which time 1182 examples had been built. Both the North Korean and Chinese air forces were supplied with La-11s and the type was used in combat during the Korean War (1950–3). By the end of that conflict, the La-11 was being phased out as a fighter by all operating air arms but a number carried on in second-line training duties into the 1960s.

TOP: **The La-11 was the end of the line for Soviet piston-engined fighters, and saw action in the Korean War.** ABOVE: **This example crash-landed in Sweden during World War II.**

Lavochkin La-11

First flight: Late 1944
Power: Shvetsov 1870hp ASh-82FNV radial piston engine
Armament: Three 23mm/0.9in cannon
Size: Wingspan – 9.95m/32ft 7.75in
Length – 8.6m/28ft 2.5in
Height – 2.95m/9ft 8in
Wing area – 17.7m²/190.53sq ft
Weights: Empty – 2770kg/6107lb
Maximum take-off – 3995kg/8807lb
Performance: Maximum speed – 690kph/429mph
Ceiling – 10,250m/33,630ft
Range – 750km/466 miles
Climb – 5000m/16,405ft in 6 minutes, 35 seconds

Lockheed F-80 Shooting Star

Lockheed began design work on a jet fighter as early as 1941 but abandoned it due to lack of the right powerplant. Work restarted in earnest in June 1943, when the British de Havilland Goblin jet engine (1361kg/3000lb thrust) became available. The first prototype was built and ready to fly in only 143 days but its maiden flight was delayed due to an engine

failure and the XP-80 finally took to the sky in January 1944. Later prototypes and the first P-80As were powered by a General Electric engine developed from Frank Whittle's W.1 turbojet. Early tests flights saw the aircraft attain speeds of 805kph/500mph, considerably faster than the piston-engined fighters in service at the time and the 660kph/410mph of the Gloster Meteor Mk 1.

ABOVE: **Too late for action in World War II, the Lockheed P-80 (later F-80) was the USA's first jet fighter.** BELOW LEFT: **The two-seater trainer version, the T-33, still flies with air forces around the world, and many are also in private hands.**

The sleek low-winged P-80 entered USAAF service in February 1945 and the first Shooting Stars, pre-production models, arrived in Italy before the end of World War II. By the end of the war a total of 45 had been delivered to the USAAF but they did not see service. The first unit solely to operate the P-80 was the 412th Fighter Group established at March Field in November 1945.

Post-war the P-80 was selected to re-equip pursuit (fighter) units of the USAAF and was the first jet fighter to be entrusted with the task of defending the USA, until being superseded by the F-86 Sabre.

In 1948, a wing of P-80As were deployed to Fürstenfeldbrück during the Berlin Airlift, in reaction to Yak-3s and La-5FNs buzzing Allied transport aircraft. As the USAF's first jet fighter, its deployment demonstrated the gravity with which the West viewed the situation. Also in 1948, the USAF (an independent service from September 1947, formerly USAAF) changed the designation of its pursuit aircraft to fighters and the P-80 became the F-80.

The last P-80A was built in December 1946 and was replaced on the production line by the much improved P-80B, which was some 454kg/1000lb heavier and powered by a better engine.

When the Korean War broke out in 1950 the F-80 was the principal USAF fighter in the theatre and ultimately the 8th,

35th, 49th and 51st Fighter Groups all flew Shooting Stars in Korea. On June 27, 1950 the first jet fighter combat involving US fighters saw four F-80s shoot down four North Korean Air Force Ilyushin Il-10 Shturmoviks.

By now the F-80C, the definitive fighter version of the Shooting Star, was in service and among other improvements offered the pilot the reassurance of an ejection seat. It was also the first USAF aircraft equipped with an explosive canopy remover. Produced in greater numbers than any other version, many earlier models were at least partly upgraded to "C" standard.

The first jet against jet air combat came on November 8, 1950, when four MiGs were seen to fly into Korean air space and were challenged by F-80Cs of the 51st Fighter-Interceptor Wing. Even though all but one of his guns jammed, Lt Russell J. Brown attacked and destroyed one of the MiGs in mid-air. In spite of this and other air combat successes, the F-80 was replaced by F-84s and F-86s during the conflict, as it had become outclassed, but it continued to serve in the fighter-bomber role.

Although the Shooting Star broke much new ground with the US Air Force, it was not widely exported, the only customers being in South America – Ecuador, Chile, Brazil, Uruguay, Colombia and Peru.

The trainer version, the two-seat T-33, was, however, widely exported and continues to serve in air arms half a century after the single-seat P-80 fighter first flew. The T-33 version was created by extending the fuselage to accommodate the two seats in tandem. Between 1949 and 1959 Lockheed built 5691 T-33s and they served with the air forces of nearly 30 countries.

TOP: **Deployed to Europe during the Berlin Airlift, the Shooting Star first fired its guns in combat during the Korean War, where it was able to hold its own for a time against the MiG-15.** ABOVE: **Tasked with defending the USA, P-80s protected their country until the arrival of the much more able F-86 Sabres.**

Lockheed F-80C Shooting Star

First flight: January 8, 1944 (XP-80)

Power: Allison 2449kg/5,400lb-thrust J33-A-35 turbojet engine

Armament: Six 12.7mm/0.5in machine-guns, plus two 454kg/1000lb bombs and eight underwing rockets

Size: Wingspan – 11.81m/38ft 9in
Length – 10.49m/34ft 5in
Height – 3.43m/11ft 3in
Wing area – 22.07m^2/237.6sq ft

Weights: Empty – 3819kg/8420lb
Maximum take-off – 7646kg/16,856lb

Performance: Maximum speed – 956kph/594mph
Ceiling – 14,265m/46,800ft
Range – 1328km/825 miles
Climb – 1524m/5000ft per minute

LEFT: **Hastily produced to defend the USA against Soviet bombers, the F-94 was derived from the T-33.** BELOW: **A battery of 48 unguided missiles gave the F-94 a powerful punch intended to knock enemy bombers from the sky.**

Lockheed F-94

When the USSR exploded its first atomic bomb in 1949, the USA quickly began to develop a range of interceptors that could tackle the expected Soviet bomber fleets. Some were to be developed for the USAF's Air Defense Command over the long term while others, such as the F-94, were rushed into production as stop-gaps.

The tandem-seat F-94 was one of the earliest radar-equipped jet fighters and eventually made up more than 24 squadrons of the fledgling US Air Defense Command, founded on 21 March 1946 to defend the USA. Based on the T-33, the F-94 was fitted with radar, carried a rear-seat observer and was armed with only four 12.7mm/0.5in machine-guns.

The prototype YF-94 first flew in April 1949 and the first production aircraft were in squadron service by the end of that year, such was the urgency to counter the perceived Soviet threat. The ADC F-94s were kept on three-minute alert for the interception of enemy bombers. With 427kg/940lb of radar kit on board, it needed an afterburner to lift off. Once airborne, the F-94 had a performance on a par with the F-80 but no better.

A total of 853 F-94s were built, and A and B models saw action in Korea,

particularly on night missions, although because of their secret radar, they were initially forbidden to overfly enemy territory. When regulations were relaxed, the F-94 began to score victories over the enemy at night and solely by use of instruments.

Named Starfire in the C variant only, the F-94C had a more powerful engine (and in turn a higher top speed), thinner wing, swept tailplane, longer fuselage and a new airborne interception radar. Armament was beefed up to 24 Mighty Mouse rockets and a further 24 housed in wing launchers. These rockets were unguided and were simply intended to destroy bombers by filling the sky with "lead". As the new generation of interceptors came into service, the F-94 was gradually retired and the type ended its brief but useful career equipping National Guard Units in the mid-1950s.

ABOVE: **This aircraft, 48-356, was the YF-94A prototype, having already served as the T-33 prototype in 1948. It is preserved in the USA at a United States Air Force base.**

Lockheed F-94

First flight: April 16, 1949 (YF-94)
Power: Pratt & Whitney 3969kg/8750lb afterburning thrust J48-P-5 turbojet engine
Armament: 24 69.85mm/2.75in Mighty Mouse air-to-air rocket projectiles, plus a further 24 housed in wing launchers
Size: Wingspan – 12.93m/42ft 5in
    Length – 13.56m/44ft 6in
    Height – 4.55m/14ft 11in
    Wing area – 31.4m²/338sq ft
Weights: Empty – 5761kg/12,700lb
    Maximum take-off – 10,977kg/24,200lb
Performance: Maximum speed – 941kph/585mph
    Ceiling – 15,665m/51,400ft
    Range – 1930km/1200 miles
    Climb – 2430m/7980ft per minute

Lockheed F-104 Starfighter

The F-104 was designed by Lockheed based on the experiences of American pilots in the Korean War – high performance was the overriding feature of this aircraft, which was frequently described as a missile with a man in it. The short wing had a maximum thickness of 10.16cm/4in and had a leading edge so sharp that when the F-104 was on the ground, it had to have a safety covering for the protection of ground crews. The Starfighter, once nicknamed "Widowmaker" because of the large number of fatal crashes of the type, found greater use with foreign air forces than with the US Air Force.

Development problems delayed the type's entry into USAF service by two years, and deliveries began in January 1958. The F-104 was the first operational fighter capable of sustained speeds above twice the speed of sound and became the first aircraft ever to hold the world speed and altitude records simultaneously. On May 7, 1958 Major Howard C. Johnson reached an altitude of 27,830m/91,243ft, and on May 16, Captain Walter W. Irwin reached a speed of 2259.3kph/1404.19mph.

On December 14, 1959, an F-104C Starfighter boosted the world's altitude record to 31,534m/103,389ft, becoming the first aircraft to take-off under its own power and exceed the 30,480m/100,000ft barrier.

The F-104G that first flew in October 1960 was an all-new version designed for the Luftwaffe as a fighter-bomber and was the most successful mark.

The US Air Force used only about one-third of the F-104s built, with most going to or being built in Canada, West Germany, Italy, Japan, Belgium, Denmark, Greece, Norway, Spain, Taiwan, Jordan, Pakistan and Turkey. In the USA, the last Air National Guard Starfighters were retired in 1975.

In 1997–8, the Italian Air Force extended the life of their licence-built F-104s to keep them flying half a century after the prototype had its maiden flight.

RIGHT: **The F-104G was a multi-role fighter-bomber version designed to meet a Luftwaffe requirement.**
BELOW: **Clearly illustrating its nickname, the sleek lines of the F-104 fuselage were very missile-like. It was the "hot ship" of its time.**

Lockheed F-104G Starfighter

First flight: March 4, 1954 (XF-104)
Power: General Electric 7076kg/15,600lb afterburning thrust J79-GE-11A turbojet engine
Armament: One 20mm/0.78in six barrel cannon, wingtip-mounted Sidewinder air-to-air missiles and up to 1814kg/4000lb of external stores
Size: Wingspan – 6.36m/21ft 9in, excluding wingtip missiles
Length – 16.66m/54ft 8in
Height – 4.09m/13ft 5in
Wing area – 18.22m²/196.1sq ft
Weights: Empty – 6348kg/13,995lb
Maximum take-off – 13,170kg/29,035lb
Performance: Maximum speed – 1845kph/1146mph
Ceiling – 15,240m/50,000ft
Range – 1740km/1081 miles
Climb – 14,640m/48,000ft per minute

General Dynamics/Lockheed Martin F-16 Fighting Falcon

The F-16 Fighting Falcon, with its origins in the 1972 USAF Lightweight Fighter Program, is one of the best combat aircraft in service today. It is highly manoeuvrable and has proven itself in air-to-air combat and air-to-surface attack. It is a relatively low-cost, high-performance weapons system used by the USAF and a number of other nations.

The single-seat F-16A first flew in December 1976 and became operational with the USAF in January 1979. The F-16B, a two-seat model, has tandem cockpits with a bubble canopy extended to cover the second cockpit. Space for the second cockpit was created by reducing the forward fuselage fuel tank size and reduction of avionics growth space. During training, the forward cockpit is used by a student pilot with an instructor pilot in the rear cockpit.

All F-16s delivered since November 1981 have built-in structural and wiring provisions and systems architecture that permit expansion of the multi-role flexibility to perform precision strike, night attack and beyond-visual-range interception missions. This improvement programme led to the F-16C and F-16D aircraft, which are the single- and two-seat equivalents of the F-16A/B, and incorporate the latest cockpit control and display technology. All active USAF units and many Air National Guard and Air Force Reserve units have converted to the F-16C/D.

The F-16 was also licence-built by Belgium, Denmark, the Netherlands and Norway – who needed to replace their F-104 Starfighters. Final airframe assembly lines were located in Belgium and the Netherlands, and these European F-16s are assembled from components manufactured in the four client countries as well as in the USA. Belgium also provided final assembly of the F100 engine used in the European F-16s. The programme increased the supply and availability of repair parts in Europe and thus improved the Europe-based F-16's combat readiness. Turkey also had an F-16 production line.

In the air combat role, the F-16's manoeuvrability and combat radius exceed that of all potential threat fighter aircraft. It can locate targets in all-weather conditions and detect low-flying aircraft in radar ground clutter. In an air-to-surface role, the F-16 can fly more than 860km/500 miles, deliver its weapons with superior accuracy while defending itself against enemy aircraft, and then return to base. The

TOP: **This early F-16 caused a stir when it visited the UK in the late 1970s. The type was a quantum leap in fighter design.** ABOVE: **The highly manoeuvrable fly-by-wire F-16 is always a favourite at air shows.**

aircraft's all-weather capability allows it to deliver ordnance accurately during non-visual bombing conditions.

In designing the F-16, advanced aerospace science and proven reliable systems from other aircraft such as the F-15 and F-111 were selected. These were combined to simplify the design process and reduce the aircraft's size, purchase price, maintenance costs and weight. The light weight of the fuselage is achieved without reducing its strength – with a full load of internal fuel, the F-16 can withstand up to 9G, which exceeds the capability of other current fighter aircraft. The cockpit and its bubble canopy give the pilot unobstructed

ABOVE: **F-16s will be in service for many years to come.** FAR LEFT: **The USAF Thunderbirds aerobatic team were a great advertisement for the type.** LEFT: **An excellent photograph of an F-16C Fighting Falcon, showing the cockpit area and to its right the exit nozzle of the internal cannon.**

forward and upward vision, and greatly improved vision over the side and to the rear while the seat-back angle was expanded from the normal 13 degrees to 30 degrees, increasing pilot comfort and gravity force tolerance. The pilot has excellent flight control of the F-16 through its fly-by-wire system, where electrical wires relay commands, replacing the usual cables and linkage controls. For easy and accurate control of the aircraft during high G-force combat manoeuvres, a side-stick controller is used instead of the conventional centre-mounted control column. Hand pressure on the side-stick controller sends electrical signals to actuators of flight control surfaces such as ailerons and rudder.

Avionics systems include a highly accurate inertial navigation system in which a computer provides steering information to the pilot. The plane has UHF and VHF radios, plus an instrument (automatic) landing system. It also has a warning system and electronic countermeasure pods to be used against airborne or surface electronic threats.

USAF F-16Cs and Ds were deployed to the Persian Gulf during 1991 in support of Operation Desert Storm, where more sorties were flown than with any other aircraft. These versatile fighters were used to attack airfields, military production facilities, Scud missile sites and a variety of other targets.

In February 1994, Italy-based USAF F-16s, deployed to help NATO keep the peace in Bosnia, engaged and destroyed Serb bombers attacking targets in central Bosnia. Turkish licence-built F-16s also enforced the No Fly Zone over Bosnia. Other F-16 operators include Bahrain, Egypt, Greece, Indonesia, Israel, Pakistan, South Korea, Portugal, Singapore, Taiwan, Thailand and Venezuela. The 4000th F-16 was delivered in May 2000 and production and upgrades will undoubtedly keep the F-16 in the front line for many years to come.

ABOVE: **Belgium was one of the European nations who engaged in a licence-build F-16 programme.**

General Dynamics/ Lockheed Martin F-16A

First flight: January 20, 1974 (YF-16)

Power: Pratt & Whitney 10,824kg/23,830lb afterburning thrust F100-PW-100 turbofan engine

Armament: One 20mm/0.78in cannon, nine hard points to carry up to 5435kg/12,000lb of air-to-air missiles, bombs and rockets

Size: Wingspan – 10m/32ft 10in, including wingtip air-to-air missiles
Length – 15.03m/49ft 4in
Height – 5.01m/16ft 5in
Wing area – 28.9m²/300sq ft

Weights: Empty – 6607kg/14,567lb
Maximum take-off – 14,968kg/33,000lb

Performance: Maximum speed – 2125kph/1320mph
Ceiling – 15,250m/50,000ft plus
Range – 580km/360 miles
Climb – 15,250m/50,000ft per minute

Lockheed Martin/Boeing F-22 Raptor

The advanced air superiority F-22 Raptor fighter was developed in response to a 1983 United States Air Force request for designs of an Advanced Tactical Fighter – a next generation, air superiority fighter. The designs of current front-line US fighter aircraft are decades old and with so much new technology now available, the US military are keen that replacement aircraft incorporate as many new developments in performance and function as possible.

The Lockheed proposal, the YF-22A, was rolled out on August 29, 1990, and first flew on September 29 having been unofficially named Lightning II, after the famous Lockheed fighter of World War II. More stealthy than the F-15, the YF-22A design was more optimized for manoeuvrability, featuring design elements such as vertical thrust vectoring engine exhausts.

The YF-22 was declared the winner of the competition in April 1991 – the first true F-22 impressive prototype was rolled out on April 9, 1997 and its first flight was on September 7, 1997. Flight tests demonstrate that the F-22 combines good handling characteristics with very high manoeuvrability and the

ABOVE: **The second F-22, pictured here on its first flight on June 29, 1998. The Raptor is considered by many to be the world's most advanced fighter.**

test program is expected to continue through 2003, with operational introduction of the Raptor scheduled for 2005.

The heart of the F-22's electronic capability is the APG-77 radar system which is able to detect an enemy aircraft's radar from distances up to 460km/286 miles. It will then acquire the enemy aircraft as a target it can kill at distances of up to 220km/136 miles – the F-22 radar signal will be very difficult to detect and the stealthy F-22 will be virtually invisible to radar.

If the enemy does manage to detect the signal, they must then get a radar lock on the F-22 to launch an attack – the F-22 radar can also analyze the enemy's radar and send out a jamming burst. Between dealing with active threats, the radar system collects information from the combat area, locates electronic systems, classifies them, and alerts the pilot to possible threats or high-priority targets. The F-22's avionics were designed to enable a lone pilot to undertake missions that normally require a two-man crew.

As a safety measure, the aircraft's eight internal fuel tanks are flooded with nitrogen to reduce the danger of fire from fuel fumes. The gas is produced by an on-board nitrogen generation system from air.

Ground crews can monitor the status of the aircraft systems through a laptop computer that can list faults, undertake diagnosis and even check the oil level.

The F-22 is constructed mainly from composites and titanium alloys. Radar absorbent materials are used to minimize the aircraft's radar signature, and the aircraft's shape is intended to make it less conspicuous to radar. The aircraft's frameless canopy is also designed to reduce radar reflections.

The cockpit control layout is based on high-intensity monitor displays, plus a holographic Head-Up Display (HUD). The cockpit also features HOTAS controls so the pilot can issue commands to the systems without releasing the flight controls.

The Pratt & Whitney F-119-PW-100 engine is very advanced but has been designed for ease of maintenance so that all components can be removed or replaced with one of six standard tools. The engine includes vertical thrust vectoring

ABOVE: **The F-22 is expected to be operational from 2005 and will be capable of achieving air superiority in the most hostile air combat situations.**
BELOW: **Pictured at Edwards Air Force Base, California, in October 1999, the F-22 incorporates all relevant new technologies.**

exhaust nozzles to improve the Raptor's manoeuvrability in low-speed combat and are automatically directed by the F-22's flight control system. The exhaust does not emit visible smoke during normal operations. The engine's supersonic cruise capability allows, without the use of afterburner, rapid location to a combat area, fast exit from the target area as a means of defence and higher launch velocities for munitions.

Despite some official doubts about the need for an advanced fighter that is estimated to cost at least $70 million a unit, the USAF plans to field 339 Raptors. The first squadron will be operational by 2005.

Lockheed Martin/ Boeing F-22 Raptor

First flight: September 29, 1990 (YF-22)
Power: Two Pratt & Whitney 16,095kg/35,438lb afterburning thrust F119-100 turbofans
Armament: One 20mm/0.78in cannon, four AIM-9 Sidewinders carried in side weapons bays. Ventral weapons bay can carry four AIM-120 AAMs or six AIM-120s. Additional ordnance can be carried on four underwing hardpoints
Size: Wingspan – 13.56m/44ft
Length – 18.92m/62ft 1in
Height – 5m/16ft 5in
Wing area – 78m^2/840sq ft
Weights: Empty – 14,395kg/31,760lb
Maximum take-off – 27,216kg/60,000lb
Performance: Maximum speed – Mach 2
Ceiling – 15,250m/50,000ft
Range and climb data not published

LEFT: **A US Navy F2H-2 Banshee – note the straight wings.**

McDonnell F2H-3 Banshee

First flight: January 11, 1947

Power: Two Westinghouse 1474kg/3250lb thrust J34-WE-34 turbojets

Armament: Four 20mm/0.78in cannon plus underwing racks for 454kg/1000lb of bombs

Size: Wingspan – 12.73m/41ft 9in
Length – 14.68m/48ft 2in
Height – 4.42m/14ft 6in
Wing area – 27.31m²/294sq ft

Weights: Empty – 5980kg/13,183lb
Maximum take-off – 11,437kg/25,214lb

Performance: Maximum speed – 933kph/580mph
Ceiling – 14,205m.46,600ft
Range – 1883km/1170 miles
Climb – 2743m/9000ft per minute

McDonnell F2H Banshee

The F2H Banshee, though similar in design and appearance to the company's earlier FH-1 Phantom, was larger and had more powerful twin Westinghouse J34 engines which gave about twice the power of the J30 engines in the FH-1.

Designed to meet the US Navy's exacting requirements for carrier operations, while also satisfying the requirement for high speed and increased rates of climb, the F2H Banshee first flew in January 1947. It became the Navy's standard long-range all-weather fighter and entered US Navy service in 1948 as their second carrier jet fighter, after the FH-1. They served with distinction with the US Navy in Korea in 1950–3 but by the end of the conflict they had been superseded by more advanced designs. That said, Banshees remained in service with US Navy reserve units until the mid-1960s.

The Royal Canadian Navy acquired 39 ex-US Navy Banshees between 1955 and 1958. A total of 805 F2H Banshees were made.

McDonnell F3H Demon

LEFT: **The F3H was planned to be the world's first missile-only fighter.**

McDonnell F3H-2 Demon

First flight: August 7, 1951 (XF3H-1)

Power: Allison 6350kg/14,000lb afterburning thrust J71-A-2E turbojet

Armament: Four 20mm/0.78in cannon and four AIM-7C Sparrow AAMs

Size: Wingspan – 10.77m/35ft 4in
Length – 17.96m/58ft 11in
Height – 4.44m/14ft 7in
Wing area – 48.22m²/519sq ft

Weights: Empty – 10,039kg/22,133lb
Maximum take-off – 15377kg/33,900lb

Performance: Maximum speed – 1041kph/647mph
Ceiling – 13,000m/42,650ft
Range – 2205km/1370 miles
Climb – 3660m/12,000ft per minute

The F3H Demon was the first swept-wing jet fighter aircraft built by McDonnell Aircraft and also the first aircraft designed to be armed only with missiles rather than guns. The carrier-based, transonic, all-weather Demon fighter was designed with the philosophy that carrier-based fighters need not be inferior to land-based fighters. However, the planned powerplant, the new J40 turbojet, failed to meet its expectations and left early Demons (F3H-1N) under-powered. Production delays were also caused by the Navy's desire for the Demon to be an all-weather nightfighter. And so, although the prototype had flown in August 1951, the radar-equipped Demon did not enter service until March 1956 as the F3H-2N and then with the Allison J71 turbojet as the powerplant.

By the time production ceased in 1959, 519 Demons had been built including the definitive Demon fighter-bomber (F3H-2). At its peak US Navy use, the Demon equipped 11 squadrons.

McDonnell F-101 Voodoo

Developed from the XF-88 prototype interceptor that first flew in 1948, the F-101 Voodoo was conceived as a long-range escort fighter for USAF Strategic Air Command B-36s. The F-101 was never going to have the range to stay with the intercontinental bombers but with the still impressive range of over 2414km/1500 miles, the Voodoo went on to a lengthy career as an interceptor and the first USAF

supersonic reconnaissance aircraft. The prototype F-101A first flew in September 1954, and after entering USAF service in 1957 the F-101 was used in a number of speed and endurance record attempts, which were intended to show the Soviets just how fast and far USAF fighters could go. On November 27, 1957, four RF-101As (reconnaissance

versions) took off from California and after refuelling in flight, two of the aircraft landed at McGuire Air Force Base, New Jersey, while the other two turned around and landed back at March Air Force Base in California on the other side of the continental United States. Meanwhile, Major Adrian Drew, flying an F-101A at Edwards Air Force Base, set a new absolute speed record of 1942.97kph/1207.34mph. All these record-breaking flights earned the Voodoo the nickname "One-Oh-Wonder".

The two-seat all-weather F-101B first flew in 1957. In service it had a Hughes fire-control system and was armed with six Falcon air-to-air missiles, or two Genie nuclear-tipped air-to-air missiles and four Falcons.

Fifty-six surplus Voodoos were transferred to the Royal Canadian Air Force in 1961 as CF-101Bs. A decade later these were replaced by more capable ex-USAF aircraft that continued in RCAF service until 1985. USAF and

RCAF Voodoos guarded the polar approaches to North America against Soviet bombers.

The last US Air Force F-101 was retired in 1971, while the last Air National Guard F-101s were retired in 1983. Reconnaissance versions of the Voodoo were also supplied to the Chinese Nationalist Air Force.

McDonnell F-101B Voodoo

First flight: September 29, 1954 (F-101A)
Power: Two Pratt & Whitney 6749kg/14,880lb afterburning thrust J57-P-55 turbojet engines
Armament: Two MB-1 Genie nuclear-tipped air-to-air missiles and four Falcon air-to-air missiles or six Falcon air-to-air missiles
Size: Wingspan – 12.09m/39ft 8in
Length – 20.54m/67ft 4.75in
Height – 5.49m/18ft
Wing area – 34.19m²/368sq ft
Weights: Empty – 13,141kg/28,970lb
Maximum take-off – 23,768kg/52,400lb
Performance: Maximum speed – 1965kph/1221mph
Ceiling – 16,705m/54,800ft
Range – 2494km/1550 miles
Climb – 11,133m/36,500ft per minute

ABOVE LEFT: **The F-101 Voodoo set a number of speed and endurance records.** BELOW: **The RF-101 was the first USAF supersonic reconnaissance platform.**

McDonnell Douglas F-4 Phantom II

One of the world's greatest ever combat aircraft, the two-seat Phantom was designed to meet a US Navy requirement for a fleet defence fighter to replace the F3H Demon and counter the threat from long-range Soviet bombers. When the F-4 proved faster than their F-104 Starfighter, the United States Air Force ordered the Phantom too.

The F-4 was first used by the United States Navy as an interceptor but was soon employed by the US Marine Corps (USMC) in the ground support role. Its outstanding versatility made it the first US multi-service aircraft flying concurrently with the US Air Force, Navy and Marine Corps. The Phantom excelled in air superiority, close air support, interception, air defence suppression, long-range strike, fleet defence, attack and reconnaissance.

The sophisticated F-4 was, without direction from surface-based radar, able to detect and destroy a target beyond visual range (BVR). In the Vietnam and Gulf Wars alone, the F-4 was credited with 280 air-to-air victories.

Capable of flying at twice the speed of sound with ease, the Phantom was loved by its crews, who considered it a workhorse that could be relied on, that could do the job and get them home safely. F-4s have also set world records for altitude (30,040m/98,556ft on December 6, 1959), speed (2585kph/1606mph on November 22, 1961) and a low-altitude

TOP: **The F-4 Phantom, a truly classic combat aircraft, served US forces until 1996.** ABOVE: **Britain's Royal Navy operated the F-4 from its carriers from 1968.**

speed record of 1452kph/902mph that stood for 16 years. Phantom production ran from 1958 to 1979, resulting in a total of 5195 aircraft. 5057 were made in St Louis, Missouri, in the USA while a further 138 were built under licence by the Mitsubishi Aircraft Co. in Japan. F-4 production peaked in 1967, when the McDonnell plant was producing 72 Phantoms per month.

The US Air Force had 2874 F-4s, while the US Navy and USMC operated 1264. A number of refurbished ex-US forces aircraft were operated by other nations, including the UK, who bought a squadron of mothballed ex-US Navy F-4Js to complement the RAF's F-4Ms.

LEFT: **The Royal Air Force operated F-4s from 1968 until 1992, including some ex-Royal Navy examples.**

Regularly updated with the addition of state-of-the-art weaponry and radar, the Phantom served with 11 nations around the globe – Australia, Egypt, Germany, Greece, Iran, Israel, Japan, South Korea, Spain, Turkey and the UK. Britain's Royal Navy and Royal Air Force both operated Phantoms from 1968 and the last RAF Phantoms were retired in January 1992. The Phantom retired from US military forces in 1996, by which time the type had flown more than 27,350,000km (around 17 million miles) in the nation's service. In May 1998, when the aircraft was celebrating 40 years in the air, the Phantom was still flying in defence of eight nations – Egypt, Germany, Greece, Israel, Japan, South Korea, Spain and Turkey. Israel, Japan, Germany,

Turkey, Greece, South Korea and Egypt have undertaken or plan to upgrade their F-4s and keep them flying until 2015, nearly 60 years after the Phantom's first flight on May 27, 1958.

LEFT: **This German Air Force F-4 is typical of the many examples bought by foreign air arms.** BELOW LEFT: **This fine study of an RAF F-4 shows the impressive weapon load that made the Phantom such a formidable fighter.**

McDonnell Douglas Phantom FGR.2 (F-4M)

First flight: February 17, 1967

Power: Two Rolls-Royce 9305kg/20,515lb afterburning thrust Spey 202 turbofans

Armament: Fighter role – Four Sky Flash or Sparrow medium-range air-to-air guided missiles, four AIM-9 Sidewinder short-range air-to-air missiles and a 20mm/0.79in rotary cannon

Size: Wingspan – 11.68m/38ft 4in
Length – 17.73m/58ft 2in
Height – 4.95m/16ft 3in
Wing area – 49.25m^2/530sq ft

Weights: Empty 14,080kg/31,000lb
Maximum take-off – 26,300kg/58,000lb

Performance: Maximum speed – 2230kph/1386mph
Ceiling – 18,300m/60,000ft
Range – 2815km/1750 miles
Climb – 9760m/32,000ft per minute

Mikoyan-Gurevich MiG-15

This formidable fighter was designed in the USSR with the benefit of swept-wing research captured from the Germans at the end of World War II. The RD-45 engine, an illegally copied Rolls-Royce Nene turbojet, was far more advanced than contemporary Russian engines and produced a performance that could outclass virtually all NATO's fighters of the time. The MiG-15 was developed for the Project S requirement for an interceptor designed to shoot down heavy bombers and was armed with one 37mm/1.45in cannon and two 23mm/0.9in cannon – German experience in World War II found that cannons larger than 20mm/0.79in were needed to bring down four-engine bombers.

The MiG-15 first flew in December 1947 but it only came to the attention of the West during the Korean War. On November 1, 1950 some USAF P-51 Mustang pilots reported coming under fire from six swept-wing jet fighters that had flown across the Yalu river from Manchuria – the Mikoyan-Gurevich MiG-15 was now in the Korean War and gave the United Nations forces a wake-up call.

After the first combat encounters with Western fighters, the MiG-15bis (improved) version appeared. Its VK-1 engine had 454kg/1000lb more thrust than the RD-45 of the earlier version, was lighter and could carry a greater fuel load. The Russian jets were starting to enjoy relatively easy victories against USAF B-29 bombers, which had previously operated in relative safety. Flying from Chinese bases immune from UN attack, the MiGs were used to defend North Korean installations and represented a major threat to UN air superiority in the north where they created the very dangerous "MiG Alley". UN aircraft could fly freely across the battlefields but faced deadly opposition when they neared areas in range of the MiG bases. The MiGs forced the B-29s to move their operations to night-time.

The USAF was quick to respond to the MiG threat by deploying the F-86A Sabre, the most modern USAF fighter available. Even so, the MiG had a better rate of climb, a tighter turning circle and a much better ceiling than the early three-cannon Sabre. The Sabre's armament of six 12.7mm/0.5in machine-guns was no match for the MiGs, although the Sabre was a steadier gun platform.

The first MiG versus Sabre dogfight took place on December 17, 1950, when four F-86s came upon four MiGs at an altitude of 7620m/25,000ft. Leader of the F-86 section, Lt Colonel Bruce H. Hinton, fired 1500 rounds of ammunition and set fire to one of the MiGs, causing it to crash.

During the Korean War, the NATO Allies were so desperate to examine a MiG at close quarters that they offered a $100,000 reward for any pilot who would defect and bring his MiG-15 with him. When a North Korean pilot, Lt Ro Kun Suk, did defect in September 1953 he was not aware of the prize but was given it anyway.

BELOW: **Developed with captured wartime German data, the MiG-15 is a classic jet fighter aircraft.**

Codenamed "Fagot" by NATO, the MiG-15 became standard equipment with Warsaw Pact air forces until the late 1960s, when it was relegated to training duties. At least 3000 single-seat MiG-15s were built in the former Soviet Union and in Czechoslovakia (as the S-102 and S-103) and Poland (as the LIM1 and 2). In addition, from 1949 over 5000 two-seat MiG-15UTIs (known as the CS-102 and LIM-3 in Czechoslovakia and Poland respectively) were built for operational conversion or training and a number remain in service at the time of writing. More than half a century after it first flew, the MiG-15 is still earning its keep.

RIGHT: **Fifty years after it first took to the air, the MiG-15 remained in service with some air arms in 2000.** BELOW: **Two preserved Korean War adversaries – the MiG-15 in the background and the F-86 Sabre in the foreground.**

MiG-15bis

First flight: December 30, 1947
Power: Klimov 2700kg/5952lb VK-1 turbojet
Armament: One 37mm/1.45in cannon and two 23mm/0.9in cannon
Size: Wingspan – 10.08m/33ft 0.75in
Length – 10.86m/35ft 7.5in
Height – 3.7m/12ft 1.75in
Wing area – 20.6m²/221.74sq ft
Weights: Empty – 3681kg/8115lb
Maximum take-off – 6045kg/13,327lb
Performance: Maximum speed – 1075kph/668mph
Ceiling – 15,500m/50,855ft
Range – 1860km/1156 miles
Climb – 3500m/11,480ft per minute

Mikoyan-Gurevich MiG-17

Design of the MiG-17, initially an improved version of the MiG-15, began in 1949 and the aircraft flew long before the MiG-15's guns were fired in anger over Korea. The development work was particularly focused on the MiG-15's poor handling at high speed and the MiG-17, a completely revised design, introduced longer more swept wings and a taller tail with a greater sweep of the horizontal surfaces.

The prototype MiG-17 first flew in 1950 and production of what NATO codenamed "Fresco-A" began in August 1951. Deliveries began in 1952 but were too late to take part in the Korean War, although in reality the first MiG-17s were not much of an improvement over the MiG-15s.

The F model (NATO codename "Fresco-C") of the MiG-17 had an afterburning engine developed from the illegally copied Rolls-Royce Nene that powered the MiG-15. This represented the first major improvement over the -15, so much so that production began in early 1953 while manufacture of the single-seat MiG-15 was stopped. The MiG-17 could carry no more fuel than the MiG-15 internally but its afterburning engine demanded rather more fuel, consequently MiG-17Fs were rarely seen without two 400 litre/88 gallon drop tanks.

Most -17s produced were F models, the only other versions produced in quantity being night/all-weather fighters developed from the earlier unsuccessful MiG-17P. The first was the MiG-17PF codenamed "Fresco-D" by NATO and equipped with search and ranging radar. In 1956 the MiG-17PFU

TOP: **Designed to replace the MiG-15, early MiG-17s had a minimal performance edge over their earlier cousin.** ABOVE: **MiG-17s remained in service as trainers into the third millennium AD.**

became the first missile-armed fighter in Soviet service, equipped with four ARS-212 (later known as AA-1) "Alkali" air-to-air missiles in place of guns. These missiles were "beam-riding", in that they were guided to a target by a radar beam aimed by the launch target.

The MiG-17 was only produced for five years in the USSR but in that time over 6000 were built, of which some 5000 were MiG-17Fs. The Fresco remained one of the most numerous fighters in Soviet service well into the 1960s and many remained in service as trainers as late as 2000.

At least 9000 MiG-17s were built, the majority of them in the USSR but with production also undertaken in Poland, where around 1000 were built as the LIM-5P. A dedicated ground-attack version known as the LIM-5M was developed in Poland, equipped for bomb-carrying and rocket-assisted take-off. China also licence-produced the MiG-17, as the J-5, well into the 1970s. Two-seat versions of the MiG-17 were only built in China as the Soviet Union believed the two-seat MiG-15 to be a perfectly adequate trainer for the MiG-17 and MiG-19. The Chinese two-seat MiG-17 was made by Chengdu (1060 built between 1966 and 1986) and designated JJ-5. The export JJ-5 was known as the FT-5.

Some Warsaw Pact nations went on to use the type in the ground-attack role, armed with bombs and rockets and the type was supplied to many other nations.

MiG-17s saw action in the Congo and in the Nigerian civil war while the Syrians also made extensive use of the MiG fighter. Perhaps the best-known combat use of the MIG-17 is, however, its actions with North Vietnam from 1965 to 1973. The Soviet fighter was a major thorn in the side of the US Air Force and Navy, whose supersonic fighters were expected to rule the skies over Vietnam. The much lighter and more agile MiG-17 could out-turn any US jet fighter and its guns were more reliable and effective than missiles in close combat. The MiG-17 gave US pilots in Vietnam a kill-to-loss ratio about four times worse than in Korea and directly led to a far-reaching evaluation of US fighter aircraft design and tactics, from which the F-16 was one result.

Often eclipsed by earlier and later MiG designs, the MiG-17 was certainly one of the greatest fighters.

ABOVE: **A number of MiG-17s are kept in flying condition by private collectors in the USA.**

ABOVE: **A preserved example at Titusville, Florida.** BELOW: **This MiG-17 has the tell-tale air intake fairing which housed the aircraft's Izumrud radar equipment.**

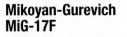

Mikoyan-Gurevich MiG-17F

First flight: January 1950

Power: Klimov 3380kg/7452lb thrust VK-1F afterburning turbojet

Armament: One 37mm/1.46in cannon, two or three 23mm/0.9in cannon plus up to 500kg/1102lb of weapons under wings

Size: Wingspan – 9.63m/31ft 7.25in
Length – 11.26m/36ft 11.25in
Height – 3.8m/12ft 5.5in
Wing area – 22.6m^2/243.27sq ft

Weights: Empty – 3930kg/8664lb
Maximum take-off – 6075kg/13,393lb

Performance: Maximum speed – 1145kph/711mph
Ceiling – 16,600m/54,460ft
Range – 1980km/1230 miles with external fuel
Climb – 5000m/16,405ft in 2 minutes, 36 seconds

Mikoyan-Gurevich MiG-19

Mikoyan-Gurevich MiG-19SF

First flight: September 18, 1953

Power: Two Tumansky 3300kg/7275lb afterburning thrust turbojets

Armament: Three 30mm/1.18in cannon, plus up to 500kg/1102lb of weapons under the wings

Size: Wingspan – 9.2m/30ft 2.25in
Length – 12.6m/41ft 4in
Height – 3.88m/12ft 8.75in
Wing area – 25m^2/269.11sq ft

Weights: Empty – 5760kg/12,699lb
Maximum take-off – 9100kg/20,062lb

Performance: Maximum speed – 1450kph/901mph
Ceiling – 17,900m/58,725ft
Range – 2200km/1367 miles with drop tanks
Climb – 6900m/22,640ft per minute

Like the MiG-17, design of the MiG-19 was underway long before the Korean War (1950–3). Reportedly on a direct order from Stalin, the MiG design bureau sought to create an all-new supersonic fighter and not just a development of an existing type. The resulting aircraft, capable of supersonic speed in level flight, was a truly great fighter.

The MiG-19, Russia's first supersonic fighter, first flew, powered by two Mikulin AM-5 turbojets (the first Soviet-designed

turbojets to be mass-produced), in September 1953 and entered service as the MiG-19P. The type was withdrawn, however, after a series of accidents due to stability problems. The redesigned

MiG-19S had an all-moving tailplane (which aided stability at all speeds) and was powered by Tumansky RD-9B turbojets, which were essentially renamed but more powerful AM-5s. Air for the engines was drawn in through what appeared to be a single nose intake but was actually split to allow each engine to draw in air through its own intake. This reduced the potential damage caused by bird strike or ingestion of foreign objects on the ground.

The -19S was delivered from mid-1955 and when production ceased in 1959, about 2500 had been built. Among the variants were the all-weather radar-equipped MiG-19PF and the MiG-19PM, armed with missiles in place of guns. NATO codenamed the MiG-19 as "Farmer".

Soviet-built aircraft were supplied to Poland and Czechoslovakia, where they were known as the LIM-7 and S-105

respectively. MiG-19s were also licence-built by the Chinese, who recognized the exceptional fighter capability of the MiG-19 and built twice as many as the USSR from 1961. Under the designation Shenyang J-6, China exported to Albania, Bangladesh, Egypt, Kampuchea (Cambodia), Pakistan, Tanzania and Vietnam. Pakistan's J-6s saw extensive combat in its war against India and J-6s were also encountered over Vietnam by US fighters.

LEFT: **This example of a MiG-19, preserved in a Russian museum, was an all-new supersonic fighter from the MiG bureau.** BELOW: **The MiG-19 was the Soviet Union's first fighter capable of supersonic flight.**

Mikoyan-Gurevich MiG-21

The MiG-21, originally designed as a short-range high-performance fighter, has, because of its hard-hitting armament and simple cost-effectiveness, become the most widely used fighter aircraft in the world. Experiences from the air war over Korea influenced the design of the delta-winged MiG-21, which was developed from a series of prototypes that flew in the mid-1950s.

The first MiG-21s (codenamed "Fishbed" by NATO) reached front-line units in the winter of 1957–8, initially armed with only two 30mm/1.18in cannon. The MiG-21F was the first major production version and was exported to the Soviet Union's Warsaw Pact allies as well as to Finland. Large numbers were also sold to Arab air forces, who used them against the Israeli Air Force in the Arab-Israeli War (1973). The MiG-21 was popular with pilots because it handled well, was highly manoeuvrable and could fly at twice the speed of sound.

Licensed production was also undertaken in Czechoslovakia and India, while China undertook major unlicensed production, having reverse-engineered (copied) examples they had acquired legitimately. Main shortcomings were limited range and endurance but the -F model came with a centreline 490 litre/108 gallon drop tank, giving the MiG longer legs.

1960 saw the development of the MiG-21PF with a redesigned nose to accommodate the new R1L radar in a moveable conical centrebody in the middle of the nose air intake. This model also introduced the more powerful R-11F2-300 engine for improved performance. Throughout its service life the -21 has been improved and upgraded, and in 2000 Romania's Aerostar were still offering upgraded MiG-21 Lancers for air defence duties, having upgraded Romanian Air Force MiG-21s. Romania was just one of many countries still operating the MiG-21 almost 50 years after the prototype first flew.

ABOVE: **This MiG-21, airbrakes deployed, is a Czech Air Force machine.** LEFT: **A MiG-21MF of the Slovak Air Force.**

Mikoyan-Gurevich MiG-21bis

First flight: Late 1957 (Production MiG-21F)

Power: Tumansky 7500kg/16,535lb afterburning thrust R-25 turbojet engine

Armament: One twin-barrel 23mm/0.9in cannon in underbelly pack and underwing provision for 1500kg/3307lb of weapons, including AA-2 or AA-8 air-to-air missiles and rocket pods

Size: Wingspan – 7.15m/23ft 5.5in
Length – 15.76m/51ft 8.5in
Height – 4.1m/13ft 5.5in
Wing area – 23m^2/247sq ft

Weights: Empty – 5200kg/11,465lb
Maximum take-off – 7960kg/17,550lb

Performance: Maximum speed – 2230kph/1385mph
Ceiling – 18,000m/59,050ft
Range – 1160km/720 miles
Climb – 17,680m/58,000ft per minute

Mikoyan-Gurevich MiG-23/-27

The disappointing range of the MiG-21 led to a 1965 requirement for a replacement fighter with considerably better endurance. An enlarged MiG-21 and the all-new Ye-23-11/1 were proposed, the latter becoming the prototype MiG-23, which first appeared at the 1967 Aviation Day flypast. Like the MiG-21 before it, the new aircraft was planned in two versions – an interceptor for use with the Soviet Union's PVO air defence forces, and a ground-attack version (the MiG-27) to serve with the USSR's tactical air forces, Frontal Aviation.

The -23 differed from previous production MiG jets by switching the air intake from a centre nose inlet to side inlets, which allowed the search radar to be accommodated in a large nose-cone. The MiG-23MF, known as "Flogger-B" by NATO, was the first production variant, entering Soviet service in 1973 and other Warsaw Pact air arms soon after.

The MiG-23 was not only the USSR's first production aircraft with a variable-geometry "swing-wing", it was also the first swing-wing fighter anywhere. It and the MiG-27 have three sweep positions – minimum (16 degrees) for take-off, low-speed flight and landing; middle (45 degrees) for cruising, and maximum (72 degrees) for high-performance flight.

The MiG-27 ("Flogger-D") fighter-bomber/attack version, can be distinguished from the MiG-23 by its different nose, which slopes away sharply from the cockpit for better pilot view, earning the nickname "ducknose" from its crews. Due to the aircraft's role as a battlefield attack aircraft, the pilot of the -27 is protected from small arms fire by armour on the side of the cockpit. Terrain-avoidance radar relieves the pilot of some of the high workload associated with low-level operations.

Among the operators of the MiG-23/-27 were Poland, Hungary, Bulgaria, East Germany, Romania and Czechoslovakia. Downgraded MiG-23s were exported outside the Warsaw Pact nations to Libya, Syria, Egypt, Ethiopia, India, Cuba, Algeria, Iraq, Afghanistan and North Korea. India's Hindustan Aeronautics produced MiG-27Ms for the Indian Air Force until 1997, finally bringing Flogger production to a close after nearly three decades, with around 4000 aircraft built. MiG-23s and -27s are, however, likely to remain potent aircraft for Russia and many of the nations listed for years to come.

In the late 1980s the US Air Force acquired some ex-Egyptian Air Force MiG-23s for realistic air-combat training of American and NATO pilots.

TOP: **Having "lit the fires", the pilot of this Czech Air Force MiG-23 prepares to accelerate away.**

ABOVE: **More than three decades after it first flew, the MiG-23 is still an effective interceptor.**

Mikoyan-Gurevich MiG-23MF

First flight: 1966

Power: Tumansky 12,500kg/27,550lb afterburning thrust R-29 turbojet engine

Armament: One 23mm/0.9in cannon in belly pod, plus five pylons for air-to-air missiles and rockets

Size: Wingspan – 14.25m/46ft 9in, spread
Length – 16.8m/55ft 1.5in
Height – 4.35m/14ft 4in
Wing area – 28m²/301.4sq ft

Weights: Empty – 11,300kg/24,912lb
Maximum take-off – 18,500kg/40,785lb

Performance: Maximum speed – 2500kph/1550mph
Ceiling – 18,600m/61,025ft
Range – 1300km/808 miles
Climb – 15,240m/50,000ft per minute

Mikoyan-Gurevich MiG-25

The MiG-25 was developed in the early 1960s to counter the threat posed to the Soviet Union by the remarkable US B-70 Valkyrie Mach 3 bomber. Although the B-70 never entered service, the MiG-25 (NATO codename "Foxbat") did and it remains the world's fastest fighter aircraft, capable of Mach 2.8 and up to Mach 3 (3200kph/2000 mph) for short periods. The West was first publicly aware of the Foxbat in April 1965, when it was announced that the prototype had set a new speed record in a 1000km/620 mile closed circuit. The prototype of the reconnaissance version had actually first flown in March 1964. The type subsequently set a number of other records, including an absolute world altitude record of 37,650m/123,524ft.

The high-speed flight environment is a hostile one and aircraft have to be made of special materials to withstand the high temperatures experienced in these operations – the MiG-25 airframe is made of nickel steel and has titanium wing and tail unit leading-edges to withstand the heat generated during very high-speed flight. The MiG-25 is no dogfighter, uses a lot of fuel quickly and needs a very long take-off and landing but it was after all a highly specialized aircraft designed for a very specific purpose – to get very high very quickly.

The interceptor version, MiG-25P, went into production first and entered service in 1970. The later MiG-25PD had look-down/shoot-down radar, more powerful engines and an infra-red search and track capability. Although the B-70 threat never materialized, the MiG-25 did, however, have another high-speed high-altitude target, the USAF SR-71 Blackbird, and it was soon stationed along the eastern and western borders of the USSR to keep the Blackbird at bay. Intercepts were directed by ground control until the powerful on-board radar could lock on to the target. Four of the world's largest, long-range missiles, the AA-6 "Acrid", could then be fired from up to 80km/50 miles away. These missiles, some 6m/19.5ft long, were specially developed to kill the B-70 and were fitted with either infra-red or radar-homing heads.

The reconnaissance MiG-25RB Foxbat entered service about the same time as the interceptor. Four aircraft were stationed in Egypt in 1971 to spy on Israeli positions and were completely immune to the Israeli F-4 Phantoms far below.

Mikoyan-Gurevich MiG-25P

First flight: March 6, 1964 (Ye-155R-1 prototype)

Power: Two Tumansky 11,000kg/24,250lb afterburning thrust R-31 turbojet engines

Armament: External pylons for four air-to-air missiles, typically four AA-6 "Acrid" air-to-air missiles or two AA-7 "Apex" with two AA-8 "Aphid" air-to-air missiles

Size: Wingspan – 13.95m/45ft 9in
Length – 23.82m/78ft 1.75in
Height – 6.1m/20ft
Wing area – 56.83m²/611.7sq ft

Weights: Empty – 20,000kg/44,090lb
Maximum take-off – 36,200kg/79,800lb

Performance: Maximum speed – 2975kph/1848mph
Ceiling – 24,385m/80,000ft
Range – 1125km/700 miles
Climb – 15,240m/50,000ft per minute

Export versions were supplied to Algeria, India, Libya, Syria and Iraq – the only confirmed Iraqi air-to-air victory of the Gulf War of 1991 was scored by a MiG-25 over a US Navy F/A-18 Hornet.

ABOVE: **The MiG-25 was developed into the MiG-31.**
BELOW: **The MiG-25 is made largely of nickel steel and titanium.**

Mikoyan-Gurevich MiG-29

Mikoyan-Gurevich MiG-29

First flight: October 7, 1977

Power: Two Klimov 8312kg/18,300lb afterburning thrust RD-33 turbojet engines

Armament: One 30mm/1.18in cannon, six underwing hardpoints carrying 3000kg/6615lb of weapons, including six AAMs or rockets and bombs

Size: Wingspan – 11.36m/37ft 3in
Length – 14.87m/48ft 9in
Height – 4.73m/15ft 6in
Wing area – 38m²/409sq ft

Weights: Empty – 10,900kg/24,030lb
Maximum take-off 18,500kg/40,785lb

Performance: Maximum speed – 2445kph/1518mph
Ceiling – 18,013m/59,060ft
Range – 3000km/1863 miles
Climb – 19,825m/65,000ft per minute

Over 1200 examples of this very capable, incredibly agile fighter have been built and the type has been exported widely. The MiG-29 was developed in the early 1970s as a high-performance, highly manoeuvrable lightweight fighter to outperform the best the West could offer. The prototype took to the air for the first time in 1977 but it

was a further seven years before the type entered service – ultimately 460 were in Russian service and the rest were exported.

Codenamed "Fulcrum" by NATO, the aircraft has been exported to Bulgaria, Germany, Cuba, Romania, Poland, Slovakia, Peru, Syria, Hungary, Iraq, India, Iran, North Korea, Malaysia and Moldova amongst others. It is not widely known, but the USA acquired 21 MiG-29s in 1997 from Moldova after Iran had expressed interest in the high-performance fighters. In a unique accord between the USA and Moldova, the aircraft were shipped to the USA to prevent them being acquired by rogue states.

The radar can track ten targets up to 245km/152 miles away and enables look-down-shoot-down capability, while the pilot's helmet-mounted sight allows him or her to direct air-to-air missiles wherever the pilot looks.

The MiG is also designed for rough-field operations – special doors seal off the main air intakes to protect against foreign object ingestion during start up and taxiing. Air is drawn in via louvres in the wingroots instead and as the aircraft takes off the inlet doors open.

The Russians have begun to upgrade some MiG-29s to MiG-29SMT standard by increasing the range and payload, new computer screens replacing cockpit instruments, as well as improved radar and inflight refuelling capability.

Daimler Chrysler Aerospace modified a number of Polish MiGs for NATO compatibility after that nation joined NATO in 1999, just as they did the East German MiG-29s after German reunification in 1990.

A navalized version, the MiG-29K, was developed but has so far not been produced.

LEFT: **Although it was designed in the early 1970s, the MiG-29 remains a very potent fighter in service around the world.** BELOW: **A fine air-to-air photograph of a Czech Air Force MiG-29.**

Mikoyan-Gurevich MiG-31

LEFT: **Derived from the formidable MiG-25, the MiG-31 is equipped with a very powerful radar.**

Mikoyan-Gurevich MiG-31

First flight: September 16, 1975 (Ye-155)
Power: Two Aviadvigatel 15,520kg/34,170lb afterburning thrust D-30F6 turbofan engines
Armament: One 23mm/0.9in cannon, four AA-9 "Amos" long-range air-to-air missiles under fuselage, two AA-6 "Acrid" air-to-air missiles and four AA-8 "Aphid" air-to-air missiles on underwing hardpoints
Size: Wingspan – 13.464m/44ft 2in
Length – 22.7m/74ft 5in
Height – 6.15m/20ft 2in
Wing area – 61.6m^2/663sq ft
Weights: Empty – 21,825kg/48,115lb
Maximum take-off – 46,200kg/101,850lb
Performance: Maximum speed – 3000kph/1863mph
Ceiling – 20,618m/67,600ft
Range – 720km/447 miles at Mach 2.3 with full armament load
Climb – 10,000m/32,810ft in 7 minutes, 54 seconds

Codenamed "Foxhound" by NATO, the very large MiG-31 was developed from the MiG-25, and replaced the Tu-128 as the main Soviet long-range interceptor. The MiG-31 and its two-man crew was designed to counter low-flying strike aircraft and cruise missiles and is able to engage targets from a considerable distance. Equipped with the long-range AA-9 air-to-air missiles, it is a most effective protector of Russian airspace.

Development began in the 1970s and the prototype MiG-31 (the Ye-155MP) first flew in 1975. The first of around 300 MiG-31s were delivered to the Soviet Air Force from 1979.

Although the Foxhound was inspired by the MiG-25, it is a new all-weather, all-altitude aircraft. Its airframe is composed of nickel steel, light alloy and titanium to cope with the rigours associated with its high performance. The aircraft's sophisticated "Flash Dance" radar, said to be the most powerful fitted to any of the world's fighters, can scan almost 200km/124 miles ahead as well as behind and below. Managed by the back-seater, it can track up to ten targets at once and simultaneously engage four of them having established which present the greatest threat.

Later models had an in-flight refuelling capability which greatly

extended the aircraft's endurance and on-board digital datalinks, allowing aircraft to exchange data about targets and tactical situations.

LEFT: **The F-2's family connections with the F-16 are clear.**

Mitsubishi F-2

First flight: October 1995
Power: General Electric 13,444kg/29,600lb afterburning thrust F110-GE-129 turbofan engine
Armament: One 20mm/0.78in cannon, plus AIM-9L Sidewinders/Mitsubishi AAM-3 air-to-air missiles on wingtips plus underwing hardpoints for weaponry including AIM-7M Sparrow air-to-air missiles
Size: Wingspan – 11.13m/36ft 6in
Length – 15.52m/50ft 10in
Height – 4.96m/16ft 4in
Wing area – 34.8m^2/375sq ft
Weights: Empty – 9525kg/21,000lb
Maximum take-off – 22,100kg/48,722lb
Performance: Maximum speed – Mach 2
Ceiling – 15,250m/50,000ft
Range – 830km/515 miles
Climb – not published

Mitsubishi F-2

The Mitsubishi F-2, formerly known as the FS-X, was developed in Japan with the help of the former General Dynamics (now Lockheed Martin) and the similarities between the F-2 and the F-16 are obvious. The type first flew in October 1995 and initial production versions were supplied to the Japan Air Self-Defence Force in 2000. Japan has ordered 130 F-2s to replace the JASDF's Mitsubishi F-1s.

The programme has, however, been dogged by technical problems and by

the time the F-2 entered service, each aircraft had cost four times more than a basic F-16.

The Japanese FS-X project was originally intended to produce an indigenous fighter aircraft but in 1987, after considerable US pressure, the F-16 was chosen as the basis of the new aircraft. The F-2 wing is 25 per cent larger than that of the F-16 and an enlarged radome houses a Japanese-designed radar. The fuselage is longer than the F-16 and the fly-by-wire system

is all-Japanese due to US reluctance to provide their fly-by-wire software.

The F-2 will initially serve in ground-attack/maritime strike roles but an air defence version is planned to replace Japan's ageing F-4 Phantom fleet.

North American F-86 Sabre

The North American Aviation Company's first jet design was begun in 1944, but following the capture of German research at the end of World War II, the XP-86 was redesigned to incorporate swept-tail surfaces and a swept wing, which would allow supersonic speeds. The prototype of the Sabre flew in 1947 and the aircraft entered service with the US Air Force in 1949. It proved faster than expected: in 1948 an early

production F-86 exceeded the speed of sound in a shallow dive, though the aircraft could not achieve this in level flight.

On November 1, 1950, some USAF Mustang pilots on a mission over Korea reported coming under fire by six swept-wing jet fighters that had flown across the Yalu river from Manchuria – the Russian-built Mikoyan-Gurevich MiG-15 was in the Korean War. The USAF were quick to respond to the MiG threat and on 8 November ordered the F-86 Sabre-equipped 4th Fighter Group from the USA to Korea. The F-86A was the most modern USAF fighter available but the Sabre's armament of six 12.7mm/0.5in machine-guns was no real match for the two 23mm/1.09in and one 37mm/1.46in cannon

ABOVE: **North American made full use of wartime German swept-wing research to produce the F-86.** LEFT: **The F-86, the USAF's most modern fighter, was sent to Korea to deal with the MiG-15 threat.**

of the MiG. USAF pilot training and tactics were, however, much better and the Sabre was able to give as much as it got.

The first MiG v. Sabre dogfight took place in December 1950, when four USAF F-86 Sabres came upon four MiGs at an altitude of 7620m/25,000ft. Leader of the F-86 group was Lt Colonel Bruce H. Hinton. He fired on the enemy jets and set fire to one of the MiGs, causing it to crash. On December 22, eight Sabres took on 15 MiGs and in the dogfights that followed from 9145m/30,000ft down to 305m/1000ft, the USAF fighter pilots destroyed no fewer than six of the MiGs. By the end of the Korean War, USAF F-86 Sabres had achieved 757 victories for 103 losses in combat.

The F-86D, virtually a complete redesign on the early Sabres, was an all-weather version fitted with the Hughes fire control system and was essentially a bomber-destroyer. The collision-course radar would take the jet to the target on autopilot and at the right moment the system would extend a box from the belly and unleash 24 70mm/2.75in unguided Mighty Mouse high explosive rockets.

The F-86E was produced from late 1950 and had an "all-flying" tail that was adjustable in flight. Canadian-built versions of the F-86E were supplied to the Royal Canadian Air Force, the RAF and the new Luftwaffe. The RAF received 460 Sabres, all of them flown to the UK in the space of 12 days in December 1952. Britain's Sabres were a much-needed stop-gap while the UK brought its own swept-wing fighters into service and enabled RAF squadrons based in West Germany, the Cold War front line, to provide a totally robust and modern fighter defence against Soviet would-be attackers. In December 1953, No.66 Squadron at Linton-on-Ouse became the first swept-wing unit of RAF Fighter Command when they swapped Meteor F.8s for F-86s. The RAF's Sabres based in West Germany were all replaced by Hunters by the end of May 1956.

Some of the Canadian-built Sabres were later passed on to Italy and Greece under NATO terms to ensure those countries' air forces were well-equipped. Italy's Fiat also licence-built the all-weather F-86K for Italy, France, West Germany, the Netherlands and Norway. For most NATO pilots, the Sabre gave them their first experience of high-speed jet flight. The very capable Sabre, so widely deployed throughout NATO, must have had some deterrence value against the USSR.

Australia's Commonwealth Aircraft Corporation also licence-built the F-86 (as the Sabre Mk 30, 31 and 32) for the Royal Australian Air Force.

The Sabre remained in production until 1957. The US Navy version, known as the FJ-2 Fury, entered service in 1952. Total Sabre and Fury production amounted to over 9500 aircraft. A number of preserved examples continue to fly.

TOP: **The all-weather D model was essentially an all-new Sabre.** ABOVE: **USAF F-86Ds were deployed for all-weather UK air defence between late 1953 and mid-1958.** BELOW: **The Sabre gave many NATO fighter pilots their first high-speed jet experience.**

North American F-86D Sabre

First flight: October 1, 1947 (XP-86)

Power: General Electric 3402kg/7500lb afterburning thrust J47-GE-17B turbojet engine

Armament: 24 70mm/2.75in unguided Mighty Mouse high-explosive rockets

Size: Wingspan – 11.3m/37ft 1in
Length – 12.29m/40ft 4in
Height – 4.57m/15ft
Wing area – 26.76m²/288sq ft

Weights: Empty – 5656kg/12,470lb
Maximum take-off – 7756kg/17,100lb

Performance: Maximum speed – 1138kph/707mph
Ceiling – 16,640m/54,600ft
Range – 1344km/835 miles
Climb – 3660m/12,000ft per minute

North American F-82 Twin Mustang

It would be easy to say that this aircraft looks as if it were made of left-over parts at the North American factory but despite its name, this aircraft was not simply two P-51s joined by a new centre wing. The F-82 (originally P-82) was conceived by North American in World War II as a dedicated long-range escort fighter for war in the Pacific. The vast distances between islands in the Pacific

required a fighter type that could fly for hours, yet have its pilot fresh for combat at any time. Development began in 1944 to provide a twin-engine, long-range bomber escort with a pilot and co-pilot/navigator, to reduce fatigue on long-range bomber escort missions.

The Twin Mustang was certainly produced quickly by using the existing P-51 powerplant and some common components including the two modified P-51H fuselages which, combined in a twin-boom configuration, carried the two pilots in separate cockpits. Deliveries of what was the last propeller-driven dayfighter acquired in quantity by the Air Force did not begin until early 1946, but although the Twin Mustang arrived too late for World War II, it had useful post-war Air Force service as an escort fighter and, most importantly, a nightfighter.

Radar-equipped F-82F and Gs were used extensively by Air Defense Command as replacements for the P-61 night-fighter and nine F-82Fs and five F-82Gs were converted as F-82H winterized interceptors for Alaska.

The F-82 had a very successful combat career in the Korean War. Japan-based F-82s were among the first

North American F-82G Twin Mustang

First flight: July 6, 1945

Power: Two Allison 1600hp V-1710-143/145 V-12 piston engines

Armament: Six wing-mounted 12.7mm/0.5in machine-guns, plus up to four 454kg/1000lb bombs under wings

Size: Wingspan – 15.62m/51ft 3in
Length – 12.93m/42ft 5in
Height – 4.22m/13ft 10in
Wing area – 37.9m^2/408sq ft

Weights: Empty – 7256kg/15,997lb
Maximum take-off – 11,608kg/25,951lb

Performance: Maximum speed – 742kph/461mph
Ceiling – 11,855m/38,900ft
Range – 3605km/2240 miles
Climb – 1150m/3770ft per minute

USAF aircraft to operate over Korea and the first three North Korean aircraft destroyed by US forces were shot down by all-weather F-82G interceptors on June 27, 1950. The type flew 1868 sorties in the Korean War before being withdrawn in February 1952.

LEFT: **Developed in World War II, the F-82 saw extensive action in Korea.** BELOW: **The unbelievable but effective configuration of the Twin Mustang – an unusual but potent fighter.**

North American F–100 Super Sabre

The Super Sabre was the world's first supersonic combat aircraft and was developed by North American from 1949 as a successor to the company's highly successful F-86 Sabre. The goal was an aircraft that could exceed Mach 1 in level flight and the F-100 was developed very quickly.

In May 1953 one of the prototypes exceeded the speed of sound on its first flight giving a taste of the performance to come. On October 29, 1953 the first production aircraft set a new world speed record of 1215kph/755mph. Although the first F-100s were delivered to the USAF in 1953, a series of catastrophic inflight failures delayed the F-100A's entry into service for another year. After the wings and fin were reworked to eradicate stability problems, 200 F-100As gave sterling service in the USAF.

The improved and more powerful F-100C and D fighter-bombers reached the Cold War front lines in 1956–7. The C model had inflight refuelling capability to extend the already impressive range

and a more powerful engine. The F-100D was built in greater numbers than any other version and carried ECM equipment as well as a low-altitude bombing system for "tossing" nuclear weapons. Two-seat and reconnaissance versions were also produced. By the time production stopped in 1959 almost 2300 Super Sabres had been built.

From 1966 to 1971 in the Vietnam War, USAF F-100s saw extensive service in the fighter, reconnaissance and ground-attack roles, flying more missions than the P-51 had in World War II.

Super Sabres retired from USAF service in 1972 but they remained in use with Air National Guard units until 1980. F-100s were supplied to Denmark, France, Taiwan and Turkey, the latter nation finally retiring the type in the mid-1980s.

TOP: **The F-100 was first delivered to the US Air Force in 1953.** ABOVE: **Extensively used in the Vietnam War, the Super Sabre flew many varied types of mission.** LEFT: **USAF F-100s were deployed to Europe in the late 1950s.**

North American F-100D Super Sabre

First flight: March 24, 1953
Power: Pratt and Whitney 7711kg/17,000lb afterburning-thrust J 57-P21 turbojet
Armament: Four 20mm/0.78in cannon plus six underwing load points for up to 3402kg/7500lb of weapons
Size: Wingspan – 11.81m/38ft 9in
Length – 15.09m/49ft 6in
Height – 4.95m/16ft 3in
Wing area – 35.77m^2/385sq ft
Weights: Empty – 9525kg/21,000lb
Maximum take-off – 15,800kg/34,832lb
Performance: Maximum speed – 1390kph/864mph
Ceiling – 13,716m/45,000ft
Range – 3210km/1995 miles with external drop tanks
Climb – 4877m/16,000ft per minute

Northrop F-5 series

The Northrop F-5 Freedom Fighter is a versatile, low cost, easy to maintain, lightweight supersonic fighter that first flew in 1959. More than 2000 of the 2700 aircraft built were widely exported to over 30 countries friendly to the USA. Deliveries to USAF Tactical Air Command for instructing foreign pilots began in April 1964 and pilots from Iran and South Korea were the first to be trained. A two-place combat-trainer

version, the F-5B, first flew in February 1964, and in 1966–7 a US Air Force squadron of F-5s flew combat missions in South-east Asia for operational evaluation purposes.

Canada and Spain undertook licence production of the F-5 – many Freedom Fighters remain in service with air forces around the world.

The improved F-5E Tiger II appeared in 1972 with more powerful J85 engines which required a wider fuselage. It had much better avionics and an air-to-air fire control radar system as well as a computerized gunsight. Like the F-5 before it, the F-5E attracted interest from foreign air forces, and some 20 foreign air arms had acquired Tiger IIs by the mid-1980s. Although the F-5 may lack all-weather capability, it is relatively cheap, easy to operate, robust and very agile. The first flight of the F-5E was on August 11, 1972 and the first USAF unit to receive the aircraft was the 425th TFS, responsible for training foreign pilots in the F-5 aircraft. Perhaps the best-known use of the Tiger II was as an aggressor aircraft for the USAF. US aggressor pilots were trained in Soviet tactics and used the F5-Es to provide a realistic "enemy" for USAF pilots training in aerial combat skills. Eventually, aggressor squadrons were used to help train pilots of friendly foreign nations. The F-5F was the two-seat combat trainer version of the F-5E. Taiwan, South Korea and Switzerland all produced the Tiger II under licence. Although F-5E production ceased in 1987, the manufacturers have offered

TOP: **This Norwegian Air Force F-5A sports a special scheme for a meet of Tiger squadrons.** ABOVE: **The Swiss Air Force was one of 20 foreign air arms that bought the F-5E.** BELOW LEFT: **This two-seat USAF F-5F shows how much ordnance could be carried by the type.**

a host of update options which should keep the Tiger II in the front line well beyond 2010.

The ultimate development of the F-5 was the F-20 Tigershark with, among other improvements, 80 per cent greater engine power. The USAF declined the aircraft and this effectively doomed the F-20's export potential.

Northrop F-5E Tiger II

First flight: July 30, 1959 (N-156F F-5 prototype)
Power: Two General Electric 2268kg/5000lb afterburning thrust J85-GE21 turbojets
Armament: Two 20mm/0.78in cannon in nose, two AIM-9 Sidewinder AAMs on wingtip launchers plus up to 3175kg/7000lb of mixed ordnance
Size: Wingspan – 8.13m/26ft 8in
Length – 14.45m/47ft 4.75in
Height – 4.06m/13ft 4in
Wing area – 17.28m^2/186sq ft
Weights: Empty – 4410kg/9723lb
Maximum take-off – 11,214kg/24,722lb
Performance: Maximum speed – 1734kph/1083mph
Ceiling – 15,790m/51,800ft
Range – 2483km/1543 miles with drop tanks
Climb – 8754m/28,700ft per minute

Northrop F-89 Scorpion

Northrop F-89D Scorpion

First flight: August 16, 1948

Power: Two Allison 3266kg/7200lb afterburning thrust J-35-A-35 turbojet engines

Armament: 104 Mighty Mouse 70mm/2.75in unguided rockets in wingtip pods or 27 rockets and three Falcon missiles

Size: Wingspan – 18.18m/59ft 8in
Length – 16.41m/53ft 10in
Height – 5.36m/17ft 7in
Wing area – 52.21m²/562sq ft

Weights: Empty – 11,428kg/25,194lb
Maximum take-off – 19,160kg/42,241lb

Performance: Maximum speed – 1024kph/636mph
Ceiling – 14,995m/49,200ft
Range – 4184km/2600 miles
Climb – 1600m/5250ft per minute

The F-89 was an all-weather jet fighter-interceptor designed to replace the P-61 Black Widow and F-82 Twin Mustang. It first flew in August 1948 and had a conventional layout but included what was for the time an unusual design feature called decelerons, a control surface that could operate as a speed brake to allow crews to get into firing position behind a target. While the pilot controlled the aircraft, the back-seat "observer" managed the

radar. The F-89 picked up the unofficial nickname "Stanley Steamer" because of the oversize main landing gear wheels that appeared to be more at home on a locomotive than a fighter.

The definitive F-89 Scorpion, and one version that was built in greater numbers than any other, was the D model, which carried 104 Mighty Mouse 70mm/2.75in unguided rockets in two enormous pods, one on each wingtip. This version also carried the APG-40 radar, which could detect target aircraft up to 80km/50 miles away. The impressive Hughes E-6 fire-control system could then instruct the autopilot on course corrections and even fire the F-89's rockets automatically when in range.

A total of 350 F-89Ds were converted to F-89Js under Project Ding Dong, which saw the aircraft equipped to carry the AIR-2A Genie, an unguided nuclear-tipped air-to-air missile. On July 19, 1957, a Genie was launched from an F-89J, marking the first and only time in history that an air-to-air rocket with a nuclear warhead was launched and detonated. Called Operation Plumb Bob, this test took place at 6100m/20,000ft over Nevada. The rocket was fired at a point approximately 4270m/14,000ft from the F-89 and the Genie covered this distance in 4.5 seconds.

The F-89 was withdrawn from active service in 1959 after protecting the USA, and especially the frozen north, for almost a decade. The last examples of the Air National Guard F-89s were retired from service in July 1969.

LEFT: **Note the F-89's twin turbojets almost "bolted on" beneath the fuselage.** ABOVE: **The F-89 was a large fighter. It protected the USA from Soviet bombers coming from the north.** BELOW: **As a design the F-89 didn't really break new ground, but it earned its keep as a Cold War all-weather interceptor for over ten years.**

Panavia Tornado ADV

The Tornado was produced by a three-nation (UK, West Germany and Italy) consortium, each of which assumed responsibility for the manufacture of specific aircraft sections. The resulting aircraft was a technological, political and administrative triumph, given the problems that had to be overcome. Each nation assembled its own air force's aircraft, and power for all was provided by Rolls-Royce-designed Turbo-Union engines. The strike Tornado was developed and entered service first, while the fighter version was sought as a replacement for the RAF's F-4 Phantoms and Lightnings. The resulting aircraft is an interceptor with a better rate of acceleration than either of these two classic jets. While it cannot manoeuvre as well as the F-16, the Tornado was not designed for manoeuvre. It was made to defend the UK Air Defence Region, a vast area stretching from the south-west approaches up to Iceland, including all of the UK, most of the North Sea, and much of the eastern Atlantic. The Tornado interceptor will be central to the UK's air defence for some years to come.

The Tornado ADV (Air Defence Variant) was designed to an RAF requirement for an interceptor that could perform unrefuelled combat air patrols 563km/350 miles from base, in all weathers and at all altitudes in a hostile electronic warfare environment. In simple terms the main mission envisaged for the Tornado interceptor was to loiter far out over the ocean, beyond the range of land-based radar, waiting to attack Soviet bombers as they approached from over the Arctic.

TOP: **The RAF's Tornado ADV is ideally suited to its primary role of defending the enormous UK Air Defence Region.** ABOVE: **Only the RAF and the Italian and Saudi Arabian air forces operate the ADV.**

Although there is 80 per cent commonality between the airframes, the ADV differs from the strike Tornado in having a 1.36m/4ft 7in longer fuselage. Its sophisticated GEC-Marconi Foxhunter radar can track up to 20 targets while scanning a search area up to 165km/100 miles distant. The chosen armament was the Sky Flash AAM and to achieve the required performance the missiles are carried in tandem semi-recessed pairs under the fuselage centreline.

The Tornado is one of a handful of combat aircraft with variable-geometry or "swing" wings. The wings can move automatically from the swept to the spread position and two interim settings to maximize the aircraft's aerodynamic performance as required at take-off, landing and in high-speed flight.

It has excellent short take-off capability which, together with its on-board Auxiliary Power Unit, makes the ADV well suited for operation from basic forward airfields.

The prototype ADV, the F.2, first flew in 1979 and the first F.2s were delivered to the RAF in November 1984. Due to delays in the development of the Foxhunter radar the aircraft only carried ballast in the nose, and subsequently a version of the radar that did not fully meet RAF standards, until 1989 when the full-specification radar was installed.

Early in production, from the 19th on the production line, all were produced as F. Mk.3s, featuring the RB199 Mk 104 engines, improved afterburners, larger drop-tanks, fully automatic wing-sweep control and provision for four Sidewinders in addition to the four Sky Flash missiles. The F.3 was also 35.5cm/14in longer than the F.2 to accommodate the new engines, carried 891 litres/200 gallons more internal fuel and an inflight refuelling probe was fitted on the port side as standard. However, on September 24, 1987 an F.3 flew direct from Canada to the BAE Systems plant at Warton in the UK without the need to refuel in flight, showing just how long the ADV's legs are.

During the 1980s the RAF Tornado F.3s also assumed the role of an AWACS aircraft as part of the RAF's Mixed Fighter Force plan. Using the Tornado's radar, the navigator was able to direct Hawk trainers towards bogeys, armed with AIM-9 Sidewinder missiles.

Although only Britain wanted the Tornado interceptor version, in 1995 Italy began leasing 24 F.3s from Britain while awaiting delivery of the Eurofighter. These aircraft were modified to carry the Italian Alenia Aspide AAM.

Saudi Arabia is the only export customer and Saudi F.3s, together with RAF ADVs, flew combat patrols throughout the Gulf War (1991) but without seeing action. RAF F.3s subsequently flew as part of the UN Operations Deny Flight/Decisive Edge over Bosnia-Herzegovina, policing the no-fly zone.

In 2000, the RAF F.3s were modified to carry the AMRAAM and ASRAAM missiles and were equipped with the Joint Tactical Information Distribution System (JTIDS), to enable the aircraft to engage multiple targets beyond visual range (BVR).

TOP: **Wings extended to generate maximum lift at take-off, the Tornado is one of the world's few swing-wing aircraft.** ABOVE: **The Tornado fighter variant will defend the UK for years to come.**

Panavia Tornado ADV/F.3

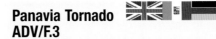

First flight: October 27, 1979

Power: Two Turbo-Union 4808kg/10,600lb (7292kg/16,075lb afterburning)-thrust RB199-34R Mk 104 turbofans

Armament: One 27mm/1.05in cannon, four Sky Flash AAMs, plus four AIM-9 Sidewinder AAMs. Italian Air Force F.3 carry Alenia Aspide AAMs instead of Sky Flash

Size: Wingspan – 13.91m/45ft 8in, spread 8.60m/28ft 3in, swept
Length – 18.68m/61ft 4in
Height – 5.95m/19ft6in
Wing area – 26.6m²/286.3sq ft, at 25 degrees sweepback

Weights: Empty – 14,500kg/31,970lb
Maximum take-off – 27,896kg/61,700lb

Performance: Maximum speed – 2381kph/1480mph
Ceiling – 21,335m/70,000ft
Range – 1853km/1150 miles intercept radius
Climb – 12,200m/40,000ft per minute

BELOW: **Although RAF Tornado fighters were deployed during the Gulf War, they did not see action.**

Republic F-84 Thunderjet/Thunderstreak

The F-84 aircraft was the USAF's first post-war fighter, and production began in June 1947. It was also the first US Air Force jet fighter capable of carrying a tactical nuclear weapon and the last USAF subsonic straight-wing fighter-bomber to enter service.

F-84s became the standard fighter-escort for USAF Strategic Air Command's bomber force and pioneered the use of aerial refuelling for fighters. During August 1953 F-84Gs, refuelled in mid-air by Strategic Air Command KC-97 tankers, were flown

7216km/4485 miles non-stop from Turner Air Force Base in Georgia, USA, to RAF Lakenheath in the UK, to demonstrate the USAF's long-range fighter-escort capability. Codenamed Operation "Longstride", this was at that point the longest non-stop mass movement of fighter-bombers in history and the greatest distance ever flown non-stop by single-engine jet fighters. F-84s had also been used in two different programmes to provide protection for B-36 Peacemaker bombers.

USAF Thunderjets saw much combat in the Korean War and entered service there in December 1950. Initially assigned to escort B-29 bombers, they were later increasingly used for ground operations. Devastating F-84 raids on dams on May 13 and 16, 1953 caused the loss of all electrical power to North Korea. During that conflict, F-84 pilots flew 86,408 missions, dropped 15,370 tonnes/50,427 tons of bombs, and managed to shoot down or damage 105 North Korean MiG-15 fighters.

The first swept-wing model, the F-84F Thunderstreak, originally designated YF-84A, was first flown on June 3, 1950 and became the only USAF production fighter derived from a straight-wing aircraft.

Under the Mutual Defense Assistance Program, some 2000 F-84s were supplied to many European air forces to bring NATO up to strength during some of the darkest days of the Cold War.

In the USA, the last straight-wing F-84s were retired from the US Air National Guard in 1957 and the last ANG F-84Fs were retired in 1971.

ABOVE: **Designed during World War II, the original straight-wing F-84 entered USAF service in 1947.**

LEFT: **The addition of swept wings in the F model extended the operational life of the F-84 – these are Royal Netherlands Air Force examples.**

Republic F-84F Thunderstreak

First flight: June 3, 1950 (YF-84A)

Power: Wright 15,917kg/7220lb-thrust J65-W-3 turbojet engine

Armament: Six 12.7mm/0.5in machine-guns, plus up to 2722kg/6000lb of external ordnance

Size: Wingspan – 10.24m/33ft 7.25in
Length – 13.23m/43ft 4.75in
Height – 4.39m/14ft 4.75in
Wing area – 30.19m^2/325sq ft

Weights: Empty – 6273kg/13,830lb
Maximum take-off – 12,701kg/28,000lb

Performance: Maximum speed – 1118kph/695mph
Ceiling – 14,020m/46,000ft
Range – 1384km/860 miles
Climb – 2257m/7400ft per minute

Republic F-105 Thunderchief

Republic F-105D Thunderchief

First flight: June 9, 1959

Power: Pratt & Whitney 11113kg/24,500lb afterburning thrust J75-P-19W turbojet

Armament: AIM-9 Sidewinder AAM, one 20mm/0.78in cannon plus up to 6359kg/14,000lb of bombs, mines and air-to-surface missiles

Size: Wingspan – 10.59m/34ft 9in
Length – 19.61m/64ft 4in
Height – 5.97m/19ft 7in
Wing area – 35.77m^2/385sq ft

Weights: Empty – 12,474kg/27,500lb
Maximum take-off – 23,967kg/52,838lb

Performance: Maximum speed – 2237kph/1390mph
Ceiling – 12,560m/41,200ft
Range – 1480km/920 miles
Climb – 10,485m/34,400ft per minute

The Republic F-105 Thunderchief is remembered as an outstanding combat aircraft which formed the backbone of United States Air Force tactical air power during the 1950s and 1960s. The F-105 was conceived in 1951 as a Republic private venture high-performance all-weather fighter-bomber to replace the F-84. The USAF,

The "Thud", as it commonly became known, was the biggest single-seat, single-engine combat aircraft in history. The F-105, developed from the YF-105A test aircraft, first entered USAF service on May 27, 1958. It was however the F-105B which was first considered operationally ready for USAF service.

The United States Air Force in Europe first received the F-105D on May 12, 1961. The first model of the Thunderchief family to possess genuine all-weather capability, the F-105D was

impressed by the design, ordered two prototypes, the first flying in October 1955. Pure fighters were becoming rarer by this time and so from the outset the F-105 was designed to carry up to 5443kg/12,000lb of mixed, possibly nuclear, ordnance, with 3629kg/8000lb of it carried in an internal weapons bay.

at the time the most sophisticated and complex type to be found in Tactical Air Command's inventory. In appearance the model of the Thunderchief was similar to the earlier F-105B, but possessed a larger nose radome. This contained a radar which permitted the F-105D to perform visual or blind

attacks with a variety of ordnance ranging from air-to-air missiles to conventional "iron" bombs.

F-105 Thunderchief's service in Vietnam was truly impressive, the type seeing action throughout the conflict but half of the 833 F-105s built were destroyed over Vietnam.

LEFT: **Before the F-84 was even in service, Republic were already working on a successor and came up with the excellent F-105.**

BELOW: **The two-seat fighter-bomber version, the F-105F, first flew in 1963.**

Saab-21

Development of the Saab-21 began in 1941 in response to a need for a Swedish-built fighter/attack aircraft to replace the various obsolete US and Italian fighters then in service with the Swedish Air Force. The resulting Saab-21 has a special place in the history books because it is the only aircraft ever to have seen front-line service propelled by piston and, later, jet power. The Daimler Benz piston-engined version, the J21A, entered service in June 1945, the only pusher-engined fighter to do so in World War II. It was fitted with an early ejection seat to meet the problem of vacating the cockpit unassisted with a snarling propeller blade some 4.58m/15ft behind.

After some problems with adapting the aircraft, the jet-engined J21RA entered service in 1949, with a top speed increase of 160kph/100mph.

LEFT: The Saab-21 had its origins as a propeller-driven aircraft.

Saab J21RB

First flight: March 10, 1947
Power: de Havilland 1500kg/3307lb-thrust Goblin 3 turbojet
Armament: One 20mm/0.78in cannon and two 13.2mm/0.53in machine-guns mounted in nose, plus two further machine-guns in wings. Provision for ventral gun pack of eight more 13.2mm machine-guns
Size: Wingspan – 11.6m/38ft 0.75in
Length – 10.45m/34ft 3.5in
Height – 2.95m/9ft 8in
Wing area – 22.2m^2/238.97sq ft
Weights: Empty – 3200kg/7055lb
Maximum take-off – 4990kg/11,001lb
Performance: Maximum speed – 800kph/497mph
Ceiling – 12,000m/39,370ft
Range – 720km/447 miles
Climb – 1400m/4600ft per minute

Ground-attack versions were produced of both powered types but the Saab-21 is fondly remembered by its pilots for being an excellent fighter, being manoeuvrable, tough and a steady gun platform.

Saab J29 Tunnan

Wartime German swept-wing research directly influenced the design of Saab's second jet fighter, which came to be named "Tunnan" (barrel) because of its shape. As Saab had no direct swept-wing experience the proposed wing for the J29 was first tested on a Saab Safir aircraft. The test worked well and the first J29 prototype, powered by a Flygmotor licence-built de Havilland Ghost, took to the air on September 1, 1948. Tunnans began to enter service in 1951 and remained in production until 1956. The J29B had larger fuel tanks, while the E model introduced an afterburner and the J29F incorporated all previous improvements. Ground-attack and reconnaissance versions were also developed.

LEFT: The name of "Tunnan" meaning "barrel" fitted the J29 perfectly.

Saab J29F

First flight: September 1, 1948 (prototype)
Power: Flygmotor 2800kg/6173lb RM2B afterburning turbojet
Armament: Four 20mm/0.78in cannon and two RB24 Sidewinder AAMs
Size: Wingspan – 11m/36ft 1in
Length – 10.13m/33ft 2.75in
Height – 3.73m/12ft 3.75in
Wing area – 24m^2/258.34sq ft
Weights: Empty – 4300kg/9480lb
Maximum take-off – 8000kg/17,637lb
Performance: Maximum speed – 1060kph/658mph
Ceiling – 15,500m/50,855ft
Range – 2700km/1678 miles
Climb – 3600m/11,810ft per minute

From 1958 the J29 was gradually replaced in Swedish Air Force units by the J32 Lansen, but in 1960 Sweden committed J29s to the UN air component that provided air cover for UN troops in the Belgian Congo. From 1961, Austria took delivery of 30 former Swedish Air Force J29Fs.

Saab J35 Draken

The remarkable Draken (dragon) was an aircraft ahead of its time and it could, if it had not been for Sweden's strict export policies, have equipped many air forces around the world. It was designed to satisfy a demanding 1949 Swedish Air Force requirement for an advanced high-performance interceptor, capable of tackling transonic-speed bombers. The specification called for speed 50 per cent greater than new fighters elsewhere, and the ability to operate from roads and other dispersed non-airfield locations. The solution was a futuristic double delta wing that gave strength with low weight and delivered all-round performance, while being able to accommodate fuel, weapons and other equipment. Before the Draken flew, its unique double delta wing was tested on a 70 per cent-scale research aircraft, which proved the viability of the design. The Draken first took to the air in October 1955 and the production version, the J35A, began to reach front-line units of the Swedish Air Force in 1960.

Among its features was a tricycle undercarriage complemented by two retractable tailwheels, deployed to permit a tail-down landing to gain the full aerodynamic braking effect of the wing. This landing technique, coupled with the use of a braking parachute, allowed the Draken to land in 610m/2000ft.

TOP: **The Draken was a front-line fighter for over three decades.** ABOVE: **The Draken's double delta-wing pianform was very advanced in its day.**

Improved versions appeared throughout the Draken's long operational life, including the J35B, with collision-course radar and increased armament, and the J35D with more powerful engines and improved avionics. The J35F had avionics that were even more advanced, an Aden cannon and the ability to carry Falcon air-to-air missiles instead of Sidewinders. The J35J upgrade of 66 J35Fs produced the ultimate Draken, to keep the type viable until the Gripen was ready to replace it from 1993. Few fighter aircraft remained as capable as the Draken for so long a period.

Reconnaissance versions (with a nose containing five cameras) and training versions were built among the total production run of 606 aircraft. Drakens were also exported to Denmark, Finland and Austria.

Saab J35F Draken

First flight: October 25, 1955

Power: Volvo 7830kg/17,262lb afterburning Volvo Flygmotor RM6C (licence-built R-R Avon 300) turbojet

Armament: One 30mm/1.18in cannon in right wing, two RB 27 and two 28 Falcon missiles, plus up to 1000kg/2205lb of bombs or rockets

Size: Wingspan – 9.4m/30ft 10in
Length – 15.35m/50ft 4.3in
Height – 3.89m/12ft 9in
Wing area – 49.2m²/529.6sq ft

Weights: Empty – 7425kg/16,369lb
Maximum take-off – 12,700kg/27,998lb

Performance: Maximum speed – 2125kph/1320mph
Ceiling – 20,000m/65,615ft
Range – 960km/597 miles with external tanks
Climb – 12,000m/39,370ft per minute

Saab Gripen

This lightweight multi-role fighter is probably the most advanced and capable single-seat fighter in service today. Designed to replace the Swedish Air Force's Viggen and Draken, the Gripen (griffin) first flew in December 1988 and employs the latest advances in aerodynamics, materials and engine technology. From the outset the designers have striven to integrate pilot and machine. The Gripen pilot receives information through an air-to-air Tactical Information Data Link System that permits real-time exchange of data within, and between, tactical air groups. Overall situational awareness is thus maximized, enabling pilots to use their aircraft weapon systems to best effect.

Cockpit ergonomics were exhaustively researched to allow the pilot the maximum amount of time for tactical operation of the aircraft. The cockpit is dominated by three large colour Multi-Function Displays and a wide-angle Head-Up Display – these four displays are the principal flight instruments. The displays are even fitted with light sensors for computer-controlled brightness.

Power is provided by a single Swedish licence-built General Electric F404-GE-400 turbofan engine, which can push the Gripen along at speeds of up to Mach 2, or, crucially, Mach 1 at any altitude. Some 20 per cent by weight of the airframe is made from carbon fibre composites. The Gripen's advanced aerodynamic configuration employs a delta wing and canard foreplanes for short-field operations and to ensure optimum agility at all altitudes, even when fully armed. This manoeuvrability is optimized by the aircraft's fly-by-wire system and the Gripen could probably outmanoeuvre all other current fighters. In these days of stealth, the Gripen has a surprisingly low radar and infra-red signature, improving its air combat survivability chances.

Central to the Gripen's targeting system is the long-range Ericsson PS-05/A multi-mode pulse-Doppler radar, which can track multiple targets simultaneously and provide rapid assessment information to the pilot. This system enables the Gripen to perform equally well in the fighter and the air-to-surface attack role. This truly remarkable aircraft's multi-role

ABOVE: **A fighter for the 21st century, the Gripen is perhaps the most advanced fighter in service today.**

TOP: **The Gripen can operate from 800m/2625ft strips, which is short for such a potent combat aircraft.**

ABOVE: **The Mach 2-capable Gripen is a much sought-after "ride" by today's fighter pilots.**

capability can be realized by the push of a button, effectively changing the Gripen's mission in mid-air.

The aircraft's flexibility is further enhanced by its ability to operate from dispersed sites, including ordinary roads and it can land and take-off from 800m/2625ft strips. An on-board auxiliary power unit allows rapid reaction times even in dispersed locations.

Considerable emphasis has been placed on maximizing component reliability and ease of access for maintenance. Fast turn-round times and in-built test equipment keeps the Gripen's time off-line to a minimum. This results in low life-cycle costs and high availability – this "force multiplier" effect has not been lost on some of the countries expressing interest in export Gripens.

The first of around 200 Gripens began operational service with the Swedish Air Force in June 1997 and the aircraft has also been ordered by the South African Air Force. The Gripen is generally acknowledged as one of the ultimate modern fighters.

Saab JAS 39A Gripen

First flight: December 9, 1988

Power: Volvo Aero Corporation/General Electric 8210kg/18,100lb afterburning thrust RM-12 turbojet

Armament: One internally mounted 27mm/1.06in cannon, one Sidewinder on each wingtip, plus five hardpoints for Sky Flash or Sidewinder AAMs, rockets or bombs

Size: Wingspan – 8.4m/27ft 6in, including wingtip launchers
Length – 14.1m/46ft 3in
Height – 4.5m/14ft 9in
Wing area – 30m²/323 sq ft

Weights: Empty – 6622kg/14,600lb
Maximum take-off – 13,989kg/30,800lb

Performance: Maximum speed – 2126kph/1321mph
Ceiling, range and climb data not published

Saab Viggen

The multi-role Viggen (thunderbolt) was designed to replace the Draken and continued Sweden's desire to remain independent of the East or West for their supply of combat aircraft. The Viggen was, for some time, the most advanced combat aircraft produced in Europe and appeared in fighter, strike and reconnaissance versions. In December 1961 the

Swedish government approved development of Aircraft System 37 which evolved into the Viggen. The basic platform was to be the AJ 37 attack aircraft, to be followed by the S 37 reconnaissance version and finally the all-weather JA 37 fighter.

Design of this ground-breaking aircraft began as far back as 1952 and by 1954 it had grown its distinctive canard wings just to the rear of the cockpit. The canards, working with the wing control surfaces, help generate additional lift during the crucial stages of landing and take-off to reduce the speeds and landing runs required to the minimum. In fact one of the essential requirements of the original specification was that the aircraft could operate from 500m/1640ft runways. Landing distance is reduced by several means – the Head-Up Display doubles as a precision landing aid, making it possible to aim just 30m/98ft in from the threshold, and the thrust reverser is interconnected with the nose gear, so that it can be selected in the air and will operate as soon as the nose is lowered.

In order to keep the aircraft as small and light as possible, it was decided to install a state-of-the-art navigational computer instead of a human navigator. The aircraft looks a lot heavier than it actually is thanks to the use of honeycomb panels in the aircraft. It is however very strong and is stressed to stand 12G in the tight turns made possible by vast wing area.

The chosen engine for the Viggen, the Pratt & Whitney JT8D-22 designed for the Boeing 727, was licence-built by Volvo in Sweden as the RM8A together with a locally designed afterburner. The fighter version however required that the engine was redesigned, at great cost, to better suit the demands of the fighter mission. The new engine, the RM8B, gave greater thrust at all altitudes and in extreme manoeuvres. The prototype first flew in February 8, 1967 and was described by the test pilot Eric Dahlstrom as being "as simple to fly as a sportsplane". In April 1968 the Swedish Government authorized Viggen production, with the first aircraft being delivered in July 1971.

LEFT: **A JA 37 Viggen, the all-weather Viggen interceptor.** BELOW: **The SF 37 Viggen reconnaissance version carries the night reconnaissance pod on the left under-fuselage pylon.**

LEFT: **The SF 37 reconnaissance version has cameras in the distinctively shaped nose.** BELOW: **The Viggen was a very advanced design, far ahead of other European types of the time.**

The aircraft was designed for simple maintenance from the outset so that conscripts with little training could turn the aircraft around quickly in readiness for its next mission. Refuelling and re-arming by seven ground personnel, of which six were conscripts, had to take less than ten minutes.

The Viggen's one-piece wrap-around windscreen was specially strengthened to survive bird strikes at high speeds and also gives the pilots an excellent forward view. Sweden's numerous dispersed underground hangars dictated that the Viggen's fin be capable of folding down for easier storage.

During the 1960s, the Swedish Air Force were expected to purchase more than 800 Viggens, but the final Viggen production total was 329 built in attack, trainer, two reconnaissance versions and the more powerful JA 37 fighter variant. The last of the Viggens, a fighter, was delivered to the Swedish Air Force in 1990. Since then the Viggen fighter has undergone several upgrades with better radar to track more targets simultaneously, new avionics and cockpit displays and extra weaponry in the form of the AIM-120 AAM.

The Viggen has been gradually replaced in Svenska Flygvapnet (Swedish Air Force) service by the Gripen.

ABOVE: **The last JA 37 interceptor version was delivered to the Swedish Air Force in 1990.** BELOW: **Able to operate from country roads and motorways, the Viggen protected Sweden for almost three decades.**

Saab JA 37 Viggen

First flight: February 8, 1967 (prototype)
Power: Volvo Flygmotor 12,750kg/28,110lb afterburning-thrust RM8B turbofan
Armament: One 30mm/1.18in cannon plus six external hardpoints for 6000kg/13,228lb of ordnance including two Sky Flash and four Sidewinder AAMs
Size: Wingspan – 10.6m/34ft 9.25in
Length – 16.4m/53ft 9.75in
Height – 5.9m/19ft 4.25in
Wing area – 52.2m²/561.89sq ft, including canards
Weights: Empty – 15,000kg/33,060lb
Maximum take-off – 20,500kg/45,194lb
Performance: Maximum speed – 2195kph/1365mph
Ceiling – 18,290m/60,000ft
Range – 1000km/620 miles
Climb – 10,000m/32,810ft in 1minute, 24 seconds

Sud-Ouest Vautour

The Vautour (vulture) was initially developed as a medium bomber in the early to mid-1950s and from a modern perspective seemed an unusual choice for development as a fighter. The advanced high-performance twin-jet design was first tested in half-scale form in 1949 and the full-scale prototypes began testing in 1951. The trials were so promising that the type, very similar in layout to the Yak-28, was rapidly developed as the S.O. 4050 multi-role combat aircraft.

Three variants of the Vautour were developed: the single-seat cannon and bomb armed Vautour IIA attack aircraft, the two-seat Vautour IIB bomber equipped with a glazed nose for the navigator/bombardier, and the Vautour IIN – the N signifying nuit, or night. The latter was a two-seat all-weather/night attack fighter equipped with an interception radar in the nose, and it took off on its maiden flight on October 16, 1952. A total of 140 examples were ordered by the French but only 70 were produced between 1957 and 1959, armed with rockets, missiles and cannon, and these were mostly based at Tours with an all-weather fighter wing. They were gradually replaced from 1973 by the Mirage F1.

In the late 1950s, Israel wanted to develop a long-range fighter capability to tackle hostile aircraft deep in enemy territory. Following evaluation flights in early 1957 the Israeli Air Force selected the Vautour to replace the de Havilland Mosquito in the long-range attack role and to counter the Arabs' Ilyushin Il-28 light jet bombers. Eighteen Vautour bombers were first exported to Israel, followed by seven of the fighter version. Capable of supersonic speed in a dive, these

TOP: **The similarities between the Vautour and the Yak-28 are clear in this photograph.** ABOVE: **The Vautour IIB bomber version equipped the French equivalent of Strategic Air Command.**

aircraft saw considerable action with the Israeli Air Force (IAF) in the 1967 Six-Day War and were in constant use until 1970.

Two IAF squadrons were equipped with the Vautour – the "Bat" squadron at Tel-Nof operated the IIN variant. The 7 IINs were initially operated as night interceptors (alongside the IAF's Meteor NF.13s until 1960 when these were retired) but after the arrival of the Mirage IIIC in 1963 they were employed as attack aircraft. They did however continue to fly night interceptions as required, for example early in 1964 when they attempted to engage Egyptian MiG-19s.

The first encounter between the IAF Vautours and the MiG-19 had occurred some five years earlier on August 16, 1959 when two Vautours engaged four Egyptian MiGs on the Israeli-Egyptian border. Later in March 1962 a single Vautour chased an Ilyushin Il-28 all the way to Damascus before being ordered to turn back.

Sud-Ouest Vautour IIN

First flight: October 16, 1952

Power: Two SNECMA 3503kg/7716lb-thrust Atar 101E-3 turbojet engines

Armament: Four 30mm/1.18in cannon, internal bomb bay with provision for up to 240 unguided rockets, plus underwing pylons for air-to-air missiles or rockets

Size: Wingspan – 15.09m/49ft 6in
Length – 15.57m/51ft 2in
Height – 4.5m/14ft 9in
Wing area – 45m²/484.4sq ft

Weights: Empty – 10,000kg/22,010lb
Maximum take-off – 20,000kg/44,093lb

Performance: Maximum speed – 1105kph/687mph
Ceiling – 15,000m/49,210ft
Range – 3200km/1990 miles
Climb – 3600m/11,800ft per minute

TOP: **This French Air Force Vautour IIN was modified to test a new radome installation.** ABOVE: **An unlikely fighter, the Vautour IIN was in front-line service with the Armée de l'Air for around 15 years.**

Sukhoi Su-9/11

The dominance of swept-wing fighters in the Korean War stimulated the ultimate development of the configuration – the delta. In the USSR, the TSAGI (National Aerodynamic Research Centre) endorsed the form and encouraged its development. Sukhoi's design bureau produced a prototype delta-winged aircraft, the T-3, and a whole range of nose configurations were tried, but it was the safe option that was chosen for the production aircraft – a circular intake with a small conical centrebody housing the radar.

Production began in 1958 and the first Su-9s joined air defence squadrons in 1959, equipped with four AA-1 "Alkali" air-to-air missiles. Two drop tanks were carried, as the internal fuel capacity of

2145 litres/472 gallons severely limited range. A special version, the T-431, set an altitude record of 28,852m/ 94,659ft in 1959. Su-9s were still in use in the early 1980s and many of the examples retired from service were converted to drones, or pilotless vehicles, and were used as aerial targets to test and train Soviet air defence personnel.

The 1961 Tushino Aviation Day display saw the first appearance of the T-43 prototype, an improved version of the Su-9. By 1965, production of the new version, by then called the Su-11, was underway with a more powerful engine, new radar and improved weaponry. The nose was lengthened and a much larger centrebody was needed to house the new Uragan 5B radar.

ABOVE: **This Su-9 was pictured at the 1967 Soviet Aviation Day display.** BELOW: **A total of 2000 Su-9/11s were built, but the Soviet Union chose to keep them all.**

The new weapons were the long-range Anab air-to-air missiles, carried in pairs, one equipped for infra-red homing (heat seeking) and the other radar-guided.

Combined Sukhoi Su-9/11 production is estimated at 2000 aircraft. None saw service with other Warsaw Pact countries and no examples of this potent fighter were exported.

Sukhoi Su-11

First flight: 1961 (T-43)

Power: Lyulka 10,000kg/22,046lb afterburning thrust AL-7F-1 turbojet

Armament: Two AA-3 Anab long-range air-to-air homing missiles

Size: Wingspan – 8.43m/27ft 8in
Length – 17.4m/57ft 1in
Height – 4.88m/16ft
Wing area – 26.2m²/282.02sq ft

Weights: Empty – 9100kg/20,062lb
Maximum take-off – 14,000kg/30,865lb

Performance: Maximum speed – 1915kph/1190mph
Ceiling – 17,000m/55,775ft
Range – 1450km/900 miles with drop tanks
Climb – 8230m/27,000ft per minute

Sukhoi Su-15

This very fast single-seat aircraft, codenamed "Flagon" by NATO, served from the 1960s into the 90s. Equipped with long-range air-to-air missiles, the Su-15 was an interceptor, whose sole role was the air defence of the USSR. Around 1500 served with Soviet PVO-Strany home defence units from 1967, deployed in areas where they were only likely to face attacking NATO bombers with little likelihood of ever having to dogfight.

Developed to replace the Su-11, the Su-15 Flagon-A was the first production version and was first seen at the 1967 Aviation Day display – it was clearly a twin-engine development of the Su-11 but with side intakes necessitated by the introduction of the large conical radome. The large rear-warning radar appeared on this model and was common to most of the Flagon family.

Flagon interceptor missions were almost always flown under ground control and this included the most infamous Su-15 mission of all, on September 1, 1983. At 03.26 local time, Su-15 pilot Major Vassily Kasmin launched two AA-3 Anab air-to-air missiles at a Korean Air Lines Boeing 747 airliner, which had strayed 400km/250 miles north of its planned route. The airliner was overflying

ABOVE: **The Sukhoi Su-15 was a very big fighter that protected the Soviet Union and Russia for around 30 years.** BELOW: **This picture of an example preserved in a Russian museum shows the size of the large nose radome.**

Soviet military installations and after reportedly firing warning shots with cannon, the Su-15, under instruction from ground control, attacked from a distance of 800m/2624ft and destroyed the airliner with the loss of all 269 passengers and crew.

The "Flagon-D" was the first version produced in large numbers and differed from the A by having bigger span wings with a kinked leading edge. The E model was also produced in quantity and was powered by more powerful engines (hence the larger air intakes), presumably to reduce the scramble time.

The "Flagon-F" was the ultimate version and entered service in 1975. It introduced bigger engines, gun pods and a more powerful radar, housed in an ogival-shaped radome designed to reduce drag and improve supersonic acceleration.

From the mid-1990s, the Su-15 was replaced by the Su-27 and MiG-31. Two-seat trainer versions and experimental versions with lift jets were also produced.

Sukhoi Su-15 Flagon-F

First flight: 1965

Power: Two Tumansky 7200kg/15,873lb afterburning thrust R-13F2-300 turbojets

Armament: Four AA-3 "Anab" medium-range air-to-air missiles carried on underwing pylons, two AA-8 "Aphid" short-range air-to-air missiles on inboard positions, plus two 23mm/0.9in gun pods

Size: Wingspan – 10.53m/34ft 6in
Length – 21.33m/70ft
Height – 5.1m/16ft 8.5in
Wing area – 36m²/387.5sq ft

Weights: Empty – 11,000kg/24,250lb
Maximum take-off – 18,000kg/39,680lb

Performance: Maximum speed – 2230kph/1386mph
Ceiling – 20,000m/65,615ft
Range – 725km/450 miles
Climb – 10,670m/35,000ft per minute

Sukhoi Su-27 family

The arrival of the long-range Su-27 (codenamed "Flanker" by NATO) gave the USSR a formidable fighter that could escort its bomber force all the way to the UK. This high-performance aircraft, which also had the capability of intercepting aircraft over long distances, came as a shock to NATO planners when it was deployed in the mid-1980s. About 20 per cent larger than the F-15 Eagle, the Su-27 is one of the biggest and most imposing fighters of all time.

Development work began in 1969 under Pavel Sukhoi himself and the prototype first flew in 1977, but early models displayed serious instability problems and it was considerably redesigned. Nevertheless, the Su-27 in service today is considered by many to be the pinnacle of Russian fighter design and the masterpiece of the Sukhoi bureau.

The fast-climbing and superbly manoeuvrable fly-by-wire Flanker can carry up to 10 air-to-air missiles, including the 112km/70-mile-range AA-10C. That amount of missiles gives the Flanker "combat persistence" – it can keep on fighting long after other fighters would have had to turn for home. Huge internal fuel tanks give very long range (up to 4000km/ 2484 miles), with no need for drag-inducing external fuel tanks.

The Su-27's Zhuk radar can track targets while continuing to scan for others and perhaps most importantly gives the aircraft a look-down/shoot-down capability. Very advanced electronics enables the Flanker to detect and destroy an enemy fighter beyond visual range (BVR) at tree-top height, without the need to descend to that level and lose a height advantage. The Su-27 equips air arms in Russia, Belarus, Uzbekistan, Ethiopia, China, Vietnam and the Ukraine

TOP: **The large Su-27 first flew in April 1981 and came as a shock to potential adversaries of the Soviet Union.** ABOVE: **Preparing to land, this Su-27 has deployed its enormous dorsal airbrake which reduces the aircraft's speed most effectively.**

– China also negotiated manufacturing rights to produce its own Su-27s, which began to appear in December 1998.

The Su-27P is a single-seat air defence fighter, the Su-27S is a multi-role version capable of carrying a 4000kg/8820lb bomb load and the Su-27UB is a two-seat operational trainer. Specially modified versions have set more than 40 altitude and climb records.

The Su-30 is a two-seat air defence fighter capable of 10-hour missions and can also serve as an airborne command post for other Su-27s. India and China have ordered these aircraft, which like the derivative Su-37, have canards and thrust-vectoring nozzles for enhanced manoeuvrability.

The Su-27 spawned a whole family of fighter aircraft, including the Su-33, Su-35 and Su-37, but the Su-27 is likely

ABOVE: **This Ukrainian Air Force example shows the huge rear defensive radar boom which effectively gives the type's pilots eyes in the back of their head.**

LEFT: **The excellent Su-27 did much to remove the advantage enjoyed in the early 1980s by US fighter types like the F-15.**

to be the mainstay of the Russian aviation industry for some years to come.

The Russian Navy's carrier arm is equipped with the Su-33 Naval Flanker version (originally the Su-27K), with moveable foreplanes plus folding wings and tailplane. Deployed since 1995 and certainly the most modern fighters in the Russian inventory, Su-33s provide the Russian Admiral Kuznetsov carrier class with air defence. Landing gear is also strengthened and as a naval aircraft it does, of course, have an arrester hook. Because of the lower approach and take-off speeds a number of other changes were made – moveable foreplanes aid manoeuvrability and control in all aspects of flight.

BELOW: **The Su-34 fighter-bomber derivative first flew in 1990, and seats its two-man crew in a side-by-side cockpit.**

Sukhoi Su-27P

First flight: April 20, 1981
(T-10S-1 pre-production prototype)
Power: Two Saturn/Lyulka 12,516kg/27,557lb
afterburning thrust AL-31F turbofans
Armament: One 30mm/1.18in cannon, plus ten
hardpoints for up to ten air-to-air missiles
from AA-8 "Aphids" to AA10Cs
Size: Wingspan – 14.7m/48ft 3in Length – 21.94m/
72ft Height – 5.93m/19ft 6in Wing area – 62m²/667sq ft
Weights: Empty – 16,380kg/36,110lb
Maximum take-off – 33,000kg/72,750lb
Performance: Maximum speed – 2500kph/1553mph
Ceiling – 18,011m/59,055ft
Range – 3680km/2285 miles
Climb – 18,312m/60,040ft per minute

TOP: **The Su-37 version has canard foreplanes and agility-enhancing thrust vectoring nozzles.** ABOVE: **The performance and agility of the Su-37 Super Flanker makes it a potent dogfight adversary.**

Sukhoi Su-35/37

A version of the Su-27 fitted with canards first flew in May 1985 and was developed into what became the Su-35. The prototype of the first true Su-35, initially designated Su-27M, had its test flight in June 1988. The single-seat Su-35 differed from the Su-27 in a number of ways, apart from the all-moving canard foreplanes. Improved engines provided greater thrust while flight control was managed by a digital fly-by-wire system that boasted quadruple redundancy, that is the systems could find four alternative routes by which to send control commands throughout the aircraft. This kind of system is an insurance against combat damage – on-board systems will simply find another route by which to pass the information.

The extremely efficient Phazotron radar can search over 100km/62 miles, track 24 targets simultaneously and has a terrain-following mode to guide the aircraft automatically over undulating landscapes. Development of this and the fly-by-wire system considerably delayed the overall programme. The Su-35 tailcone also houses a radar, which scans and protects the aircraft's rear. The aircraft is equipped for inflight

refuelling and auxiliary fuel tanks are fitted in the two tailfins. The cockpit Electronic Flight Information System (EFIS) consists of three TV screens and a Head-Up Display (HUD).

The Su-37 Super Flanker is a further improvement on the Su-35 and has two-dimensional thrust-vectoring nozzles controlled by the fly-by-wire system. The improved cockpit has a sidestick controller and four LCD multifunction displays. When the Su-37 appeared at the 1996 Farnborough air show piloted by Sukhoi test pilot Eugeny Frolov, it stole the show with the astounding manoeuvres made possible by thrust vectoring. The Su-37 was flipped on its back while flying at 350kph/217mph so that it faced the opposite direction, inverted and almost stationary. After pausing for two seconds (long enough to loose off a missile in combat) the thrust vectoring was used to complete the 360 degree rotation and the aircraft moved off in its original direction of flight at only 60kph/37mph.

Sukhoi's chief designer Mikhail Simonov is so confident about the

advantage bestowed by the aircraft's thrust vectoring system, that he challenged any US aircraft to a mock dogfight "… any time, any place!" At the time of writing, the Su-37 was yet to be ordered into production.

Sukhoi Su-35

First flight: June 28, 1988

Power: Two Lyulka 12,500kg/27,557lb AL-31M turbofans

Armament: One 30mm/1.18in cannon and 14 hardpoints to carry a range of missiles and bombs up to 6000kg/13,228lb

Size: Wingspan – 14.7m/48ft 2.75in
Length – 22.2m/72ft 10in
Height – 6.36m/20ft 10in
Wing area – 46.5m^2/500sq ft

Weights: Empty – 17,000kg/37,479lb
Maximum take-off – 34,000kg/74,956lb

Performance: Maximum speed – 2500kph/1550mph
Ceiling – 18,000m/59,055ft
Range – 4000km/2484 miles
Climb – not published

Supermarine Attacker

The Supermarine Attacker was designed to an RAF specification and combined a Nene jet engine with the laminar wing and landing gear of the piston-engined Spiteful. This approach was taken to bring another British single-seat jet fighter into service as soon as possible. Although the prototype first flew in July 1946, the type did not enter service until August 1951 and then with the Royal Navy, who maintained interest in the Attacker long after the RAF abandoned it. The Attacker was an unremarkable aircraft and the tailwheel made deck landing difficult, but as the first Fleet Air Arm jet fighter in front-line use, the Attacker provided the Royal Navy with its first foothold in the jet age. The type was phased out of front-line use in 1954.

LEFT: **The tail-dragging straight-winged Attacker was the Fleet Air Arm's first front-line jet fighter.**

Supermarine Attacker F. Mk I

First flight: July 27, 1946
Power: Rolls-Royce 2271kg/5000lb-thrust Nene 3 turbojet
Armament: Four 20mm/0.78in cannon in wing
Size: Wingspan – 11.25m/36ft 11in
　Length – 11.43m/37ft 6in
　Height – 3.02m/9ft 11in
　Wing area – 21m²/226sq ft
Weights: Empty – 3826kg/8434lb
　Maximum take-off – 5539kg/12,211lb
Performance: Maximum speed – 950kph/590mph
　Ceiling – 13,715m/45,000ft
　Range – 950km/590 miles
　Climb – 1936m/6350ft per minute

Attackers were also supplied to the Pakistani Air Force, who operated them as land-based aircraft.

Supermarine Scimitar

This large and heavy fighter was the Royal Navy's first swept-wing single-seat fighter and was also the first Fleet Air Arm aircraft equipped to carry an atomic bomb. The Scimitar was equally at home carrying out low-level bombing attacks, high-altitude interception with air-to-air missiles and long-range fighter reconnaissance – it represented a quantum leap from the lacklustre Sea Hawk which it replaced as the Navy's standard single-seat strike fighter.

The first operational squadron equipped with this very capable combat aircraft was No.803, formed at Lossiemouth in June 1958. Although only 76 were produced, the Scimitars gave the Royal Navy real punch and retained their nuclear role until 1969.

LEFT: **The Scimitar was a large twin-engined fighter and although only produced in limited quantities, it served the Royal Navy well in a variety of roles for a decade.**

Supermarine Scimitar F.1

First flight: January 11, 1957
Power: Two Rolls-Royce 5105kg/11,250lb static thrust Avon 202 turbojets
Armament: Four 30mm/1.18in cannon, wing pylons for up to 96 air-to-air rockets or a range of other stores
Size: Wingspan – 11.33m/37ft 2in
　Length – 16.87m/55ft 4in
　Height – 5.28m/17ft 4in
　Wing area – 45.06m²/485sq ft
Weights: Empty – 10,869kg/23,962lb
　Maximum take-off – 15,513kg/34,200lb
Performance: Maximum speed – 1143kph/710mph
　Ceiling – 14,020m/46,000ft
　Range – 2288km/1422 miles
　Climb – 3660m/12,000ft per minute

Supermarine Swift

In 1946 Britain's Air Ministry asked manufacturers to propose a replacement for the Gloster Meteor. Supermarine's entry was a development of its Attacker, but featuring staged improvements including swept wings and tail, tricycle undercarriage and a Rolls-Royce Avon engine, which became the Swift F. Mk 1. This aircraft was allocated, on a very restricted basis, to No.56 Squadron RAF in February 1954 but only to gain air experience with swept wings. High-speed and high-altitude manoeuvrability and control problems persisted with interim marks, but the FR. Mk 5 did enter RAF front-line service, equipping Nos.2 and 79 Squadrons in RAF

LEFT: The Swift was the first swept-wing jet fighter in service with the Royal Air Force, but continued problems led to premature retirement of the type.

Supermarine Swift F. Mk 1

First flight: August 5, 1951
Power: Rolls-Royce 3406kg/7500lb-thrust Avon RA7 turbojet
Armament: Two 30mm/1.18in cannon
Size: Wingspan – 9.85m/32ft 4in
Length – 12.64m/41ft 5.5in
Height – 3.8m/12ft 6in
Wing area – 28.43m²/306sq ft
Weights: Empty – 5678kg/12,500lb
Maximum take-off – 7721kg/17,000lb
Performance: Maximum speed – 1110kph/690mph
Ceiling – 13,725m/45,500ft
Range – 1175km/730 miles
Climb – 3752m/12,300ft

Germany from 1955 until 1961. This version of the Swift, an effective fighter reconnaissance aircraft, was the first reheat-engined swept-wing aircraft in RAF service.

LEFT: The Tu-28P is the largest interceptor ever built, and is some 8.4m/27ft longer than the F-14 Tomcat. This example, complete with dummy AA-5 missiles, is preserved in a Russian museum.

Tupolev Tu-28P

First flight: 1957
Power: Two Lyulka 11,200kg/24,690lb afterburning thrust AL-21F turbojets
Armament: Four AA-5 "Ash" long-range air-to-air missiles
Size: Wingspan – 18.1m/59ft 4.5in
Length – 27.2m/89ft 3in
Height – 7m/23ft
Wing area – 80m²/861sq ft
Weights: Empty – 25,000kg/55,125lb
Maximum take-off – 40,000kg/88,185lb
Performance: Maximum speed – 1850kph/1150mph
Ceiling – 20,000m/65,615ft
Range – 5000km/3105 miles
Climb – 7500m/25,000ft per minute

Tupolev Tu-28

Codenamed "Fiddler" by NATO, this very large fighter provided the USSR with a long-range fighter capability from the 1960s until its gradual replacement by Su-27s and MiG-31s in the late 1980s. The Tu-28, designed to intercept Western missile-carrying aircraft before they had a chance to launch their deadly weapons, was the world's largest all-weather interceptor. With a range of more than 3000km/1865 miles, the Tu-28 was deployed to protect the northern Soviet Union and was armed with four AA-5 "Ash" air-to-air missiles.

Production began in the early 1960s and the type entered service in the mid-1960s, although it was unknown to the West until Soviet Aviation Day in 1967. Two crew were carried in tandem.

The aircraft were phased out of service by 1992.

Vought F7U Cutlass

TOP: **Like the Douglas Skyray, the Cutlass was designed with the benefit of data derived from German wartime aerodynamic research. This Cutlass is preserved at the Museum of Naval Aviation at Pensacola in Florida.**
ABOVE: **An F7U-1 Cutlass.** BELOW LEFT: **The Cutlass is surely one of the oddest-looking fighters ever.**

In 1945 the US Navy issued a requirement for a 965kph/600mph carrier-borne fighter. German wartime aerodynamic research data proved very useful to US aircraft designers in the immediate post-war years. Vought (or Chance Vought as it was then known) designers were particularly interested in the work carried out by the Arado company on tailless aircraft and this led directly to the rather unconventional F7U Cutlass, which had a 38-degree swept wing, twin tail fins but no conventional tail surfaces. The Cutlass helped the US Navy break new ground – it was the first supersonic production aircraft in the US Navy inventory.

The F7U-1 was the first version in service but only 14 were built and these were used for trials and training. The aircraft was very demanding in terms of maintenance and it also had a high accident rate but it was very popular with pilots and could pull 16G manoeuvres when making use of its excellent aerobatics.

The F7U-3 that ultimately equipped 13 US Navy and Marine Corps squadrons ashore and on carriers was not just modified and improved – it was effectively a new design. The F7U-1 version had not been considered robust enough for carrier use so the new model was considerably tougher, being re-stressed throughout. To reduce maintenance time over 100 extra doors and access panels were added. The nose was redesigned, twice, to improve pilot visibility and the tricycle undercarriage nosewheel was both lengthened and strengthened. This new version was introduced into US Navy service from 1954 and the

F7U-3M variant was equipped to carry four laser-beam-riding Sparrow air-to-air missiles.

Most were withdrawn from service in 1956–7 as new, more capable aircraft became available. The F7U-3 was just as accident-prone as the F7U-1, with an incredible 25 per cent of all aircraft built being lost in accidents.

Vought F7U-3 Cutlass

First flight: September 29, 1948 (XF7U-1 prototype)
Power: Two Westinghouse 2767kg/6100lb afterburning thrust J46-WE-8A turbojet engines
Armament: Four 20mm/0.78in cannon, plus underwing attachments for rockets
Size: Wingspan – 12.09m/39ft 8in
Length – 13.13m/43ft 1in
Height – 4.46m/14ft 7.5in
Wing area – 46.08m^2/496sq ft
Weights: Empty – 8260kg/18,210lb
Maximum take-off – 14,353kg/31,642lb
Performance: Maximum speed – 1094kph/680mph
Ceiling – 12,190m/40,000ft
Range – 1062km/660 miles
Climb – 3960m/13,000ft per minute

Vought F-8 Crusader

The single-seat Crusader naval fighter began life as Vought's response to a 1952 US Navy requirement for a carrier-based supersonic fighter. The prototype first took to the air in March 1955 and exceeded Mach 1 during this initial flight, making it the first fighter designed for shipboard operation to fly faster than sound.

Carrier operations require that aircraft have very robust landing gear, an arrester hook, and folding wings but these features all add to the overall weight and thus can compromise performance.

Vought came up with a brilliant variable-incidence wing, which on take-off and landing could be pivoted up seven degrees. This gave the wing a high angle-of-attack and so reduced approach and take-off speeds. The raised centre section of the wing also acted as a speed brake to reduce landing speed further.

The armament consisted of four 20mm/0.78in cannon, two of the guns on either side of the fuselage. Behind the guns, on each side of the aircraft, was a launch rail for a single Sidewinder air-to-air missile. There were no wing stores pylons on the prototype, but these came on later production models.

The first production version of the F8U-1 Crusader, as it was then named, flew at the end of September 1955 and the US Navy accepted its first operational F8U-1 on December 28, 1956. The US Navy was eager to show off its new fighter and a series of speed and endurance records were bagged by Crusaders in 1956–7. On July 16, 1957 an F8U-1 and an F8U-1P reconnaissance model attempted to set a coast-to-coast speed record. The pilot of the F8U-1P that landed in New York after a flight of 3 hours and 23 minutes was Major John Glenn, later an astronaut and US senator.

The F8U-1E had an improved radar system that gave it limited all-weather capability while the more powerful F8U-2 incorporated a further improved radar and fire-control system, as well as an uprated J57-P-16 engine with 7670kg/16,900lb of afterburning thrust.

Next version was the F8U-2N, with new avionics, including a push-button autopilot, and the uprated J57-P-20 engine, with increased afterburning thrust of 8,170kg/18,000lb. Yet more versions followed. The first F8U-2NE flew at the end of June 1961 and carried an improved search and fire-control radar system for enhanced all-weather operation.

In September 1962, the US Navy introduced an aircraft designation system in line with US Air Force designations, so

ABOVE: **The last of the gunfighters – two US Navy Vought F-8 Crusaders, the top one flying in an inverted position.** BELOW: **The F-8's innovative variable-incidence wing reduced take-off and landing speeds.**

ABOVE: **The French Aéronavale was the main overseas customer for the Crusader, and operated the type until 2000.**

existing Crusader variant designations were changed. The F8U-1 became the F-8A and the later models changed thus: F8U-1E/F-8B, F8U-2/F-8C, F8U-2N/F-8D, F8U-2NE/F-8E, F8U-1P/RF-8A.

One final new-production model was built – the F-8E(FN), built for the French Aéronavale. However, French carriers were smaller than American carriers, and this dictated new engineering, including blown flaps to reduce the aircraft's landing speed.

The Aéronavale operated 42 Crusaders from the carriers *Clémenceau* and *Foch*. The French aircraft also had the capability to carry two Matra R.530 air-to-air missiles and eventually four Matra Magic R.550 heat-seeking missiles, in place of Sidewinders.

The Crusader was used by both US Marine and US Navy detachments during the war in Vietnam, its combat début coming on August 2, 1964. North Vietnamese patrol boats attacked the US Navy destroyer *Maddox* so four Crusaders from the carrier *Ticonderoga* attacked and sank one of the

patrol boats. The Marines used the aircraft largely in the attack role, but the US Navy used the Crusader as a dogfighter and in the period 1966–8 shot down at least 18 MiGs.

The Crusader proved so effective that in 1966 a re-engineering programme was established to refurbish and improve the type. Stronger wings and main landing gear plus blown flaps (devised for the French Crusaders) were added to a total of 446 rebuilt.

By 1972, fighter versions of the F-8 were being phased out of US Navy service but in 1978, 25 refurbished US Navy F-8Hs were sold on to the Philippine Air Force as F-8Ps, which finally retired in 1986. The Aéronavale Crusaders were the last of the type in service and were replaced by the Rafale from 2000, bringing more than four decades of Crusader service to an end.

ABOVE: **US Navy F-8s proved to be formidable dogfighters during the Vietnam War.**

LEFT: **The F-8 Crusader was one of the first supersonic fighters, and was a potent combat aircraft for over four decades.**

Vought F-8E Crusader

First flight: March 25, 1955
Power: Pratt & Whitney 8165kg/18,000lb afterburning thrust J57-P-20A turbojet engine
Armament: Four 20mm/0.78in cannon, four AIM-9 Sidewinder air-to-air missiles, or two AGM-12B Bullpup missiles
Size: Wingspan – 10.72m/35ft 2in
Length – 16.61m/54ft 6in
Height – 4.8m/15ft 9in
Wing area – 32.52m²/350sq ft
Weights: Empty – 9038kg/19,925lb
Maximum take-off – 15,422kg/34,000lb
Performance: Maximum speed – 1800kph/1120mph
Ceiling – 17,983m/59,000ft
Range – 966km/600 miles
Climb – 17,374m/57,000ft in 6 minutes

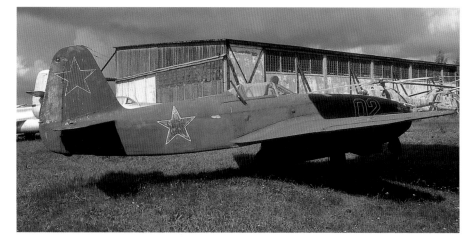

LEFT: **The Yak-17 was the penultimate Yak jet fighter modified from an original piston-powered type.**

Yakovlev Yak-17

First flight: Early 1947
Power: Klimov 1000kg/2205lb thrust RD-10A turbojet
Armament: Two nose-mounted 23mm/0.9in cannon
Size: Wingspan – 9.2m/30ft 2.25in
Length – 8.78m/28ft 9.75in
Height – 2.1m/6ft 10in
Wing area – 14.85m²/159.85sq ft
Weights: Empty – 2430kg/5357lb
Maximum take-off – 3323kg/7326lb
Performance: Maximum speed – 750kph/466mph
Ceiling – 12,750m/41,830ft
Range – 717km/446 miles
Climb – 5000m/16,405ft in 5.8 minutes

The Yak-17 was developed from the earlier Yak-15 which itself had been a conversion of the taildragging Yak-3 piston fighter. The Yak-15 had been the first successful Soviet jet fighter in service having first flown in April 1946. About 200 Yak-15s were built before being succeeded by the much improved Yak-17 of which around 430 were built.

The Yak-17 differed from the Yak-15 by having a retractable tricycle under-carriage (thus eliminating the archaic tailwheel), and a more powerful engine. Structural strengthening also took place, and to improve the aircraft's range, drop-tanks were introduced too. A two-seat conversion trainer variant (YaK-17UTI) was also built.

The Yak-17 was also operated by Poland and Czechoslovakia and was phased out by all air forces by 1955.

LEFT: **The Yak-23 took the Yak-15 design as far as it could go.**

Yakovlev Yak-23

First flight: June 17, 1947
Power: Klimov 1590kg/3505lb thrust RD-500 turbojet
Armament: Two nose-mounted 23mm/0.9in cannon plus one 60kg/132lb bomb
Size: Wingspan – 8.73m/28ft 7.75in
Length – 8.12m/26ft 7.75in
Height – 3.31m/10ft 10.3in
Wing area – 13.5m²/145.32sq ft
Weights: Empty – 2000kg/4409lb
Maximum take-off – 3036kg/6693lb
Performance: Maximum speed – 975kph/606mph
Ceiling – 14,800m/48,555ft
Range – 1200km/745 miles
Climb – 2041m/6693ft per minute

The Yak-23 was the ultimate development of the Russian Yak-15/-17 family. It differed from the Yak-17 by having the horizontal tail surfaces mounted higher up a much larger fin.

Designed as a lightweight day fighter, the Yak-23 first flew in June 1947 with power provided by an imported Rolls-Royce Derwent. It entered production,

powered by a Soviet copy of the Derwent (the RD-500), in early 1948. 310 were built and many were operated by other Eastern Bloc nations including Bulgaria, Romania, Czechoslovakia and Poland. The last of the barrel-bodied Yaks, this aircraft was always seen as a back up for the advanced swept wing fighters under development at the time

and this wonderfully agile fighter was indeed replaced throughout the Warsaw Pact by the MiG-15 in the mid-1950s.

LEFT: **The Yak-25, equipped with a heavyweight nose radar.**

Yakovlev Yak-25

First flight: June 19, 1952 (Yak-120)
Power: Two Tumansky 2633kg/5798lb-thrust RD-9 turbojet engines
Armament: Two 37mm/1.46in cannon
Size: Wingspan – 11m/36ft 1in
  Length – 15.67m/51ft 5in
  Height – 4.32m/14ft 2in
  Wing area – 28.94m^2/311.51sq ft
Weights: Empty – 7300kg/16,095lb
  Maximum take-off – 10,900kg/24,030lb
Performance: Maximum speed – 1090kph/677mph
  Ceiling – 14,000m/45,900ft
  Range – 2730km/1696 miles
  Climb – 3000m/9800ft per minute

Yakovlev Yak-25

Codenamed "Flashlight" by NATO, the two-seat Yak-25 (not to be confused with the Yak-25 single-engine fighter prototype of 1947) was the Soviet Union's first all-weather radar-equipped jet fighter and took to the air in prototype form (Yak-120) in June 1952. The new aircraft was designed to loiter for up to 2½ hours and carry the new Sokol radar that weighed in at around 500kg/1100lb. Power was provided by two jets slung beneath a swept but untapered wing. Sole armament was a pair of 37mm/1.46in cannon housed under the fuselage.

Although production began in 1953, with the aircraft then designated Yak-25, the radar was not ready for service until late 1955. The type was deployed to protect the far north of the Soviet Union against NATO bombers, and the introduction of the Yak-25 was enough to persuade the USAF that overflights of the USSR were no longer an easy reconnaissance option.

Production ceased in 1958 after 480 had been built. It remained in front-line use until the mid-1960s.

LEFT: **The Yak-28 was a multi-role type, and appeared in a number of versions.**

Yakovlev Yak-28PM

First flight: March 5, 1958 (Yak-129)
Power: Two Tumansky 6128kg/13,492lb after-burning thrust R-11AF-2-300 turbojets
Armament: Two Anab missiles, one infra-red and one radar-homing, plus two short-range air-to-air missiles
Size: Wingspan – 11.64m/38ft 2.25in
  Length – 20.65m/67ft 9in
  Height – 3.95m/12ft 11.5in
  Wing area – 37.6m^2/404.74sq ft
Weights: Maximum take-off – 15,700kg/34,612lb
Performance: Maximum speed – 1890kph/1174mph
  Ceiling – 16,000m/52,495ft
  Range – 2630km/1634 miles
  Climb – not known

Yakovlev Yak-28

At first glance the Yak-28 was similar to the Yak-25 in configuration but it was a wholly new design that first flew in prototype form during 1958 as the Yak-129. First versions developed were bomber/tactical attack aircraft but the Yak-28P was a dedicated all-weather interceptor with tandem cockpits for the two crew. It was designed to operate at low and medium altitude equipped with an Orel radar and armed with two air-to-air missiles, one radar-homing and one beam-riding.

Codenamed "Firebar" by NATO, the Yak-28 was capable of transonic flight and entered service in the winter of 1961–2. The aircraft was upgraded in numerous ways – its engines were uprated to have 6128kg/13,492lb after-burning thrust each and two short-range air-to-air missiles were added to the stores options, gaining the aircraft the designation Yak-28PM. Production ceased in 1967 after 437 fighters had been built and the type was phased out of service in the mid-1980s.

Acknowledgements

The author would like to give special thanks to Mike Bowyer, Peter March, Kazuko Matsuo and Hideo Kurihara for their help with picture research.

The publisher would like to thank the following individuals and picture libraries for the use of their pictures in the book (l=left, r=right, t=top, b=bottom, m=middle, um=upper middle, lm=lower middle). Every effort has been made to acknowledge the pictures properly, however we apologize if there are any unintentional omissions, which will be corrected in future editions.

Aerospace Publishing: 82t.

BAE Systems: 2–3; 4; 8–9; 10b; 16t; 17t; 24t; 25bl; 25br; 32t; 33lm; 33b; 58t; 69um; 103m; 128.

B.J.M. & V. Aviation: 87t.

Michael J.F. Bowyer: 31m; 34t; 34b; 35t; 36b; 37t; 37m; 38t; 39m; 39b; 41b; 44b; 45m; 45b; 46t; 47lm; 47b; 50b; 51m; 53um; 53b; 57m; 57b; 63b; 65m; 67lm; 68m; 76b; 77t; 78t; 78b; 82b; 85t; 97t; 97m; 98t; 99b; 101tl; 101tr; 103b; 104t; 104b; 109t; 111b; 122t.

Francis Crosby Collection: 55b; 74b.

Ken Duffey: 114b.

Chris Farmer: 40t; 42b; 48t; 49b; 67um; 71m; 71b; 90b.

Imperial War Museum Photograph Archive: 7t (TR 38450); 7m (CT 442); 12b (A 32268); 13br (A 31917); 14 (CT 62); 17m (CT 68); 18 (CT 72); 21t (CT 391); 23t (CT 57); 28b (CT 800); 29b (A 32830); 33um (CT 440); 35b (GLF 1082); 37b (GLF 1003); 54tr (ATP 15053C); 55t (Imperial War Museum Duxford); 55mr (A 34406); 56bl (COL 50); 56br (CAM 1473); 61 (CT 816); 68b (CT 915); 69t (CT 913); 69m (CT 916); 69lm (ATP 21301B); 70t (ATP 13595C); 85b (CT 70); 123m (A 33984); 127 (TR 38450).

Cliff Knox: 11m; 15bl; 19b; 21b; 44t; 50t; 51b; 60t; 62t; 71t; 79ml; 84t; 87lm; 92b; 94t; 97b; 103t; 107t; 110b; 111t; 116t; 117b; 122b.

Kokujoho Magazine: 41t; 65b; 76tr; 95b; 118b.

Andrew March: 91b.

Daniel J. March: 19lm; 52b; 68t; 118t.

Peter R. March: 6t; 6b; 10t; 11t; 12t; 13tr; 13bl; 16b; 19t; 19um; 20t; 20b; 21m; 22t; 23b; 25t; 26–7; 28t; 30t; 30m; 30b; 31b; 32b; 33t; 38b; 39t; 40b; 42t; 43t; 43b; 45t; 46b; 47t; 47um; 48b; 49tr; 49m; 51t; 52t; 53t; 53lm; 54b; 56t; 57t; 58b; 59t; 59m; 59b; 60m; 62bl; 62br; 64m; 64b; 65t; 67b; 69b; 70b; 72b; 73t; 74t; 75t; 76tl; 77b; 79t; 79mr; 79b; 80; 81t; 81b; 83t; 83b; 84b; 85m; 86; 87um; 87b; 88t; 88b; 89t; 89m; 90t; 91t; 92t; 93t; 93b; 94b; 95t; 96t; 96b; 98b; 99t; 99m; 100t; 100m; 100b; 101b; 102t; 102b; 105t; 105b; 106t; 107b; 110t; 111um; 111lm; 112t; 113b; 115t; 115b; 116b; 117t; 117m; 119t; 119b; 120t; 120b; 121t; 123t; 123b; 124t; 124b; 125t; 125b.

Martin-Baker Aircraft Company: 24b.

Ministry of Defence: 29t.

Northrop Grumman: 63t; 64t.

Bruce Robertson: 31t; 54tl; 54m; 60b; 72t; 73b; 75b; 89b; 106t; 112b; 114t; 121m; 121b.

Rolls-Royce: 15br.

Saab: 1; 7b; 11b; 17b; 108; 109b; 126.

Geoff Sheward: 36t; 49tl; 66; 67t; 113t.

Brian Strickland Collection: 55ml.

USAF: 22b; 35m.